Lord, Hear Our Prayer

Lord, Hear Our Prayer

Prayer of the Faithful for Sundays, Holy Days, and Ritual Masses

Year A
Year B
Year C

Jay Cormier

A Liturgical Press Book

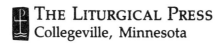 THE LITURGICAL PRESS
Collegeville, Minnesota

1   2   3   4   5   6   7   8   9

Library of Congress Cataloging-in-Publication Data

Cormier, Jay.
    Lord, hear our prayer : prayer of the faithful for sundays, holy
days, and ritual masses : year A, year B, year C / Jay Cormier.
        p.   cm.
    ISBN 0-8146-2166-X
    1. General intercessions—Catholic Church—Liturgy—Texts.
2. Catholic Church—Liturgy—Texts. 3. Catholic Church—Prayer
books and devotions—English.   I. Title.
BX2015.62.C67 1995
264'.023—dc20   95-13674
                                                                        CIP

For the Parish Community
of St. Mark the Evangelist,
Londonderry, New Hampshire

CONTENTS

INTRODUCTION

Three years ago this parishioner "inherited" the task of composing the weekly text for the Prayer of the Faithful. The first few weeks he consulted a published collection and a monthly missalette resource guide but quickly abandoned them and composed a weekly series of intercessions after reflecting on the Lectionary readings assigned for the day.

The result of that experience is this book. Let it be noted at the outset that collections like these are endeavors of questionable value. As the name implies, the Prayer of the Faithful belongs to the *faithful*, the entire worshiping community—that unique group of individuals gathered around a particular altar, who bring to that community of prayer their own experiences of joy and sorrow. It is, therefore, rather presumptuous to suggest that a single set of words could or should be used in every parish or community every Sunday.

This collection has been published as a help to other parishes and communities in developing and articulating their own prayers for the Sunday Liturgy. The pattern followed here is that which has been adapted by the Roman Church from the Eastern practice of prayers offered by the worshiping community:

- the presiding celebrant's brief invitation to the community to pray for the needs of the Church, the community, and the world;
- a series of intercessions read by the deacon, cantor, or other minister;
- the community's affirmation of these intercessions by its sung or spoken response: *Kyrie eleison*; "Lord, hear our prayer," etc.
- a concluding collect offered by the presiding celebrant.

The local community is encouraged to make these prayers their own: adapting them, rewriting them, editing them, setting them to music. Nor should the user of this book assume that the Scripture readings that are the basis of these prayers have been completely mined for ideas, imagery, and language that a community can use to articulate their prayers to God. One's own experience of time and perspective of place can find new inspiration for prayer and petition in the Sunday pericope.

With these disclaimers in mind, a few suggestions are offered:

As *General Instruction of the Roman Missal* (no. 45) notes: "In the general intercessions or prayer of the faithful, the people, exercising their priestly function, intercede for all humanity." Intercessions are offered "for the Church, for civil authorities, for those oppressed by various needs, for all people, and for the salvation of the world." This instruction has two implications for the worshiping community:

First, the Prayer of the Faithful is a prayer of *intercession*, recognizing our need and the need of all humankind for the grace of God. The Prayer of the Faithful, then, is not the time for prayers of thanksgiving or praise; it is a time for petition, our humble pleading that God enliven us with grace and wisdom, raise us up when we fall, heal us in our brokenness.

Second, the Prayer of the Faithful calls us to see beyond ourselves and our immediate community. When we celebrate the Eucharist we become united not only as a worshiping community around this altar, but we become united with the whole Church, living and dead: ". . . .by your Holy Spirit, gather all who share this one bread and one cup into the one body of Christ, a living sacrifice of praise" (Eucharistic Prayer 4). This enlarged, universal vision of the Eucharist should also enlarge the scope of our prayers beyond our personal and parochial concerns. God inspires us to pray for people we do not know and may not want to know, to pray for things we might never consider praying for or would just as soon God not grant.

To this end, in the Prayers of the Faithful in this collection, the first petition is always for the local Church and parish; the second petition is usually for those who lead and serve our Church and our nation; the third petition prays for the nations and peoples of the world; the fourth and following petitions pray for the specific needs of others (e.g., families, the poor, the sick). The final petition is always offered for those who have died; the petitions conclude with an invitation to pray those special, silent prayers each one of us possesses and offers "in the silence of our hearts."

Just as the lectors should prepare the Scriptures they will read, the deacon or reader of the petitions should prepare the texts of the Prayer of the Faithful. A stumbling, tentative reading of the petitions hardly inspires the community to pray. To this end, the text in this book has been broken down into sense lines for the reader and, in some places, key words that should be emphasized are printed in italics. The best advice that can be given to readers is to practice reading these texts *out loud* to become familiar with the wording, pace, and structure of these prayers.

Thomas More offered this prayer: *Give us, O Lord, the grace to work for the things we pray for.* The intercessions in this book were written with the great English saint's words in mind: we not only ask God's help and blessing but we commit ourselves to use that grace to bring about the "coming of your kingdom."

Jay Cormier

YEAR A

"Come, let us climb the Lord's mountain." Isaiah 2:1-5

It is now the hour for you to wake from sleep; . . . the day draws near.
Romans 13:11-14

"Stay awake! . . . You cannot know the day your Lord is coming."
Matthew 24:37-44

As we begin this season of hope and anticipation, let us confidently raise our hearts and voices in prayer:

- That our parish community's prayer and work together
  may reflect the light of Christ:
  let us pray to the Lord.

- That the leaders of Churches and governments
  may be inspired by the Spirit of God
  to make Isaiah's prophecy of "swords [turned] into plowshares"
  a reality in our time:
  let us pray to the Lord.

- That the nations and peoples of the world
  may climb together and discover
  the peace of the Lord's holy mountain:
  let us pray to the Lord.

- That all pastors, teachers, and counselors
  may "instruct" those entrusted to their care
  in the ways of reconciliation, humility, and peace:
  let us pray to the Lord.

- That this Advent season may be a time,
  not for thoughtless celebration or mindless consumerism,
  but for the renewal and re-creation of human hearts:
  let us pray to the Lord.

- [That . . .:
  let us pray to the Lord.]

- That God will welcome into "the Lord's house"
  the souls of our deceased relatives and friends
  [especially _____ *]:*
  let us pray to the Lord.

- That God will grant, in kindness and mercy,
  the prayers we now make in the silence of our hearts
  [Pause . . .]:
  let us pray to the Lord.

Come, Lord, and redeem us.
Heal us with your peace,
teach us in your ways of justice and mercy,
and unite us in your love.
We ask this in the name of Jesus, Emmanuel.

A shoot shall sprout from the stump of Jesse.   Isaiah 11:1-10

Accept one another, then, as Christ accepted you.   Romans 15:4-9

(The theme of John's preaching) "Reform your lives! The reign of God is at hand."
          Matthew 3:1-12

Emmanuel—"God is with us."
In joyful hope, then, let us pray:

- For the Church and our parish community,
  that, in the living out of our own baptism,
  we may be heralds of Christ's coming:
  let us pray to the Lord.

- For our bishops, priests, and deacons,
  and for all who serve the Church,
  that they may proclaim
  in their ministries of teaching and healing
  the coming of God's kingdom:
  let us pray to the Lord.

- For those who lead and govern,
  that the Lord's Spirit of wisdom, knowledge, and justice
  may rest upon them:
  let us pray to the Lord.

- For all Christian Churches and faith communities,
  that they may glorify God with one heart and one voice:
  let us pray to the Lord.

- [For . . .,
  that . . .:
  let us pray to the Lord.]

- For the poor, the homeless, and the forgotten,
  that we may recognize, in them, the person of Christ:
  let us pray to the Lord.

- For all the faithful who have died
  [especially _____],
  that Christ will welcome them into his Father's presence:
  let us pray to the Lord.

- For the prayers we now make in the silence of our hearts
  [Pause . . .]:
  let us pray to the Lord.

Lord God, hear the prayers of your people
who anxiously await your coming.
Help us to straighten the crooked roads of our lives
that we might create a highway
for you to enter our homes and hearts
with the peace of Christ Jesus, your Son,
in whose name we offer you these prayers.

The desert and the parched land will exult . . . and bloom. Isaiah 35:1-6, 10

See how the farmer awaits the precious yield of the soil. . . . You, too, must be patient.
James 5:7-10

"Go back and report to John what you hear and see." Matthew 11:2-11

Let us now offer our prayers in joyful hope to the Lord,
who comes to heal and save us:

- That our Church and parish community
  may be joyful messengers of the Lord's coming:
  let us pray to the Lord.

- That all nations, states, and governments
  may secure justice for the oppressed
  and a share in the earth's abundance for the poor:
  let us pray to the Lord.

- That this Christmas season
  may be a time of healing and reconciliation
  with those from whom we are estranged and separated:
  let us pray to the Lord.

- That we might bring the life of Christ
  to the deserts of despair
  and the parched lands of hopelessness
  within our homes and communities:
  let us pray to the Lord.

- [That . . .:
  let us pray to the Lord.]

- That those who fear, who suffer, and who mourn
  may discover, in our compassion and help,
  the healing presence of God:
  let us pray to the Lord.

- That Christ the Redeemer will raise up
  all who have died in his peace
  [especially _____]:
  let us pray to the Lord.

- That God will grant the prayers we now make
  in the silence of our hearts
  [Pause . . .]:
  let us pray to the Lord.

Gracious God, hear our prayers.
Come and transform our lives and our world
    from barrenness to harvest,
    from sickness to wholeness,
    from division to completeness,
    from death to life.
We offer these prayers to you
in the name of Jesus, Emmanuel.

The virgin shall be with child, . . . and shall name him Emmanuel.   Isaiah 7:10-14

You . . . have been called to belong to Jesus Christ.   Romans 1:1-7

"Joseph, son of David, . . . it is by the Holy Spirit that [Mary] has conceived this child."
Matthew 1:18-24

In joyful anticipation of the Lord's coming at Christmas,
let us join our hearts and voices in prayer:

- For our Church and parish community,
  that the Advent spirit of joyful hope
  may inspire our worship and work together
  in every season of the year:
  let us pray to the Lord.

- For all who minister to the Church,
  that they may be faithful to God's call to discipleship:
  let us pray to the Lord.

- For married couples experiencing difficult times,
  that God will give them patience and trust
  to renew their love for one another:
  let us pray to the Lord.

- For parents and guardians,
  that they may love their children
  as God the Father loves all his children on earth:
  let us pray to the Lord.

- For those who do not celebrate Christ's birth,
  that they, too, may know
  the joy and peace of the Messiah's coming:
  let us pray to the Lord.

- [For . . .,
  that . . .:
  let us pray to the Lord.]

- For all who have died
  [especially _____ *],*
  that the new life of the Messiah may be theirs:
  let us pray to the Lord.

- For the prayers we now make in the silence of our hearts
  [Pause . . .]:
  let us pray to the Lord.

Come, Lord God,
shatter the darkness of our world
with the light of your love.
Hear the prayers we offer to you,
and give us the courage and conviction
to make these prayers a reality.
We pray to you in the name of our hope,
Jesus, the Christ.

VIGIL MASS

As a bridegroom rejoices in his bride so shall your God rejoice in you. Isaiah 62:1-5

(Paul's sermon at Antioch) God has brought forth from [David's] descendants Jesus, a savior for Israel. Acts 13:16-17, 22-25

(The angel appears to Joseph) "[Mary] is to have a son and you are to name him Jesus because he will save his people from their sins." Matthew 1:1-25

MASS AT MIDNIGHT

A child is born to us, a son is given us. Isaiah 9:1-6

The grace of God has appeared, offering salvation to all. Titus 2:11-14

This day in David's city a savior has been born to you, the Messiah and Lord. Luke 2:1-14

MASS AT DAWN

Say to daughter Zion, your savior comes! Isaiah 62:11-12

God our Savior . . . saved us because of his mercy. Titus 3:4-7

[The shepherds] went in haste and found Mary and Joseph, and the baby lying in the manger. Luke 2:15-20

MASS DURING THE DAY

The Lord comforts his people, he redeems Jerusalem. Isaiah 52:7-10

In this, the final age, [God] has spoken . . . through his Son, . . . the reflection of the Father's glory. Hebrews 1:1-6

The Word became flesh and made his dwelling among us. John 1:1-18

In the peace of this holy season, let us pray:

- For our Church, the people of God,
  that the light of Christ may illuminate our life together:
  let us pray to the Lord.

- For the nations and peoples of the world,
  that the Sun of Justice may dawn upon all lands:
  let us pray to the Lord.

- For our parish family,
  that our work and worship together
  may celebrate Christ's presence among us:
  let us pray to the Lord.

- For all children and young people,
  that they may know the joy of Jesus' coming
  every day of their lives:
  let us pray to the Lord.

- [For . . .,
  that . . .:
  let us pray to the Lord.]

- For the poor, the suffering, and the forgotten,
  and for those who must spend this day alone,
  that in the miracle of Christ's birth
  they may experience the healing and hope of God:
  let us pray to the Lord.

- For all who have died in the peace of Christ
  [especially _____],
  that they may be reborn in the life of the Risen Savior:
  let us pray to the Lord.

- For the prayers we now offer to our Heavenly Father
  in the silence of our hearts
  [Pause . . .]:
  let us pray to the Lord.

Gracious God,
your love knows no limit, your compassion no end.
Hear the prayers we make
as we celebrate your most perfect gift
to your human family:
the Messiah, Jesus Christ,
who lives and reigns with you
and the Holy Spirit as the one God,
for ever and ever.

The Lord sets a father in honor over his children; a mother's authority he confirms.
Sirach 3:2-6, 12-14

Let the word of Christ, rich as it is, dwell in you. Colossians 3:12-21

YEAR A:
Joseph got up and took the child and his mother and left that night for Egypt.
He stayed there until the death of Herod. Matthew 2:13-15, 19-23

YEAR B:
(Simon's prophecy) ''This child is destined to be the downfall and the rise of many in
Israel.'' Luke 2:22-40

YEAR C:
[Mary and Joseph] returned to Jerusalem in search of him. Luke 2:41-52

Let us now join our hearts and voices in prayer
to our Father in heaven
for the needs of every member of our human family:

- For our Church and parish community,
  that Christ's peace and a dedication to thankfulness
  may reign in our life together:
  let us pray to the Lord.

- For parents, guardians, and teachers,
  that they may always realize
  the preciousness of the young lives in their care:
  let us pray to the Lord.

- For children and young people,
  that they may learn and grow in wisdom and grace
  within the joy of a loving family:
  let us pray to the Lord.

- For children who are lost and abandoned
  and for children who have been abducted,
  that, through God's loving providence,
  they will return to their homes quickly and safely:
  let us pray to the Lord.

- For families in crisis,
  for families in mourning,
  for families estranged and separated,
  that Christ may be present to them
  in the loving support of neighbors and friends:
  let us pray to the Lord.

- [For . . .,
  that . . .:
  let us pray to the Lord.]

- For all our family members and friends who have died
  [especially _____],
  that they may live in the presence of God forever:
  let us pray to the Lord.

- For the prayers we now make in the silence of our hearts
  [Pause . . .]:
  let us pray to the Lord.

Hear the prayers of your family
gathered around your table, O Lord.
As Jesus taught us to call you "Father,"
may we learn to respect and love one another
as brothers and sisters.
We offer these prayers in the name of your Son,
Jesus, the Christ.

(The Lord's blessing upon Israel) Numbers 6:22-27

You are no longer a slave but a son! Galatians 4:4-7

Mary treasured all these things and reflected on them in her heart. Luke 2:16-21

As the gift of a new year dawns,
let us come before the Lord in prayer
for the peace and safety of all people:

- For our Church and parish community,
  that our work and prayer together this year
  may bring the reign of God a step closer to fulfillment:
  let us pray to the Lord.

- For Pope N., Bishop N., Father N.,
  and for all who serve the Church,
  that, through their ministries,
  the mercy and graciousness of God may shine upon us:
  let us pray to the Lord.

- For the nations and peoples of the world,
  that all of us may recognize one another
  as sons and daughters of our Father in heaven:
  let us pray to the Lord.

- For all families and households,
  that this new year may be a time of health and happiness:
  let us pray to the Lord.

- [For . . .,
  that . . .:
  let us pray to the Lord.]

- For the poor, the suffering, and the forgotten,
  that, with our unconditional love and support,
  this new year may be an opportunity
  for them to rebuild their lives:
  let us pray to the Lord.

- For our deceased relatives and friends,
  especially those who have died in the past year,
  that the graciousness of God may shine upon them forever:
  let us pray to the Lord.

- For the prayers we now offer in the silence of our hearts
  [Pause . . .]:
  let us pray to the Lord.

Father in heaven, Lord of all beginnings,
hear the prayers we make for ourselves
and for all members of our human family.
May this new year be a new beginning for each one of us,
a new opportunity for us
to welcome your grace and peace into our lives.
May your gift of this new year
be a time of our re-creation in your life and love.
In Jesus' name, we pray.

Before all ages, in the beginning, the Most High created me, and through all ages I shall not cease to be.   Sirach 24:1-4, 8-12

May the Father enlighten your innermost vision that you may know the great hope to which he has called you.   Ephesians 1:3-6, 15-18

The Word became flesh and made his dwelling among us, and we have seen his glory.
                                                            John 1:1-18

The Word of God has made his dwelling place among us.
Rejoicing in his presence, let us pray:

- That, in embracing the Gospel of Christ Jesus,
  we may be "holy and blameless in God's sight"
  and worthy of our call to be sons and daughters of God:
  let us pray to the Lord.

- That Pope N., Bishop N., Father N.,
  and all bishops, priests, deacons, and ministers
  may be faithful and effective witnesses
  of God's Word in our midst:
  let us pray to the Lord.

- That the light of God's holy wisdom
  may illuminate every land and nation of the earth:
  let us pray to the Lord.

- That the spirit of Christmas peace
  may dwell within all hearts and homes
  in every season of every year:
  let us pray to the Lord.

- [That . . .:
  let us pray to the Lord.]

- That the sick, the poor, the struggling, and the despairing
  will discover, in our compassion and care,
  the healing presence of God:
  let us pray to the Lord.

- That all the faithful who have died
  [especially _____]
  may know the ''great hope'' to which we have been called—
  the eternal life of the Resurrection:
  let us pray to the Lord.

- That the Father of enduring love will hear the prayers
  we now offer in the silence of our hearts
  [Pause . . .]:
  let us pray to the Lord.

Hear the prayers of the people you have called,
O God of graciousness.
Open our hearts and spirits
to behold the great light of your enduring love
that dawned upon the earth
in the birth of your Son, Jesus Christ,
your Word made flesh,
in whose name we offer these prayers.

Rise up in splendor, Jerusalem! Your light has come. Isaiah 60:1-6

In Christ Jesus the Gentiles are now co-heirs with the Jews . . . of the promise.
Ephesians 3:2-3, 5-6

The star which [the astrologers] had observed . . . came to a standstill over the place where the child was. Matthew 2:1-12

Christ our Light has dawned upon the world.
In joyful hope, then, let us pray:

- That, in our work and worship together,
  our Church and parish community may reveal
  God's living presence in our world:
  let us pray to the Lord.

- That all nations and peoples
  may walk together by the light of God's peace:
  let us pray to the Lord.

- That all Churches and faith communities
  may honor and respect one another
  as co-heirs and sharers of God's promise:
  let us pray to the Lord.

- That the happiness and love
  shared by families and households during this holy season
  may be celebrated in all seasons of the new year:
  let us pray to the Lord.

- [That . . .:
  let us pray to the Lord.]

- That all who are experiencing despair and pain
  may discover the peace and healing of the Shepherd of Israel:
  let us pray to the Lord.

- That all who have died in the peace of Christ
  [especially _____]
  may live forever in the light of the Risen Messiah:
  let us pray to the Lord.

- That God will hear the prayers we now offer
  in the silence of our hearts
  [Pause . . .]:
  let us pray to the Lord.

Father,
ever present to your people in everything that is good,
hear our prayers.
May your peace and justice be the star we follow
in our lives' journey to your everlasting kingdom.
We ask this in the name of your Light and Word to us,
Jesus Christ.

Here is my servant, . . . my chosen one. Isaiah 42:1-4, 6-7

(Peter's sermon to Cornelius' household) "This is . . . 'the good news of peace' proclaimed through Jesus Christ who is Lord of all." Acts 10:34-38

(Jesus' baptism in the Jordan by John) YEAR A: Matthew 3:13-17
YEAR B: Mark 1:7-11
YEAR C: Luke 3:15-16, 21-22

To God, the Giver of life and the Author of all holiness,
let us offer our prayers:

- That, through our work and worship together,
  our parish community may be a light to our world:
  let us pray to the Lord.

- That those who proclaim the gospel
  through their ministries of teaching, healing, and charity
  may bring sight to those who are blind to the life of God
  and liberation to those imprisoned by darkness:
  let us pray to the Lord.

- That the nations and peoples of the world
  may work together for the "victory of justice":
  let us pray to the Lord.

- That we may be always faithful to our covenant with God,
  a covenant sealed in the waters of our baptism:
  let us pray to the Lord.

- [That . . .:
  let us pray to the Lord.]

- That the sick and the suffering,
  the poor and the forgotten,
  the lost and the troubled
  may find hope in the "good news of peace":
  let us pray to the Lord.

- That those who have died
  [especially _____]
  may rise to the new life of the Risen Christ:
  let us pray to the Lord.

- That the God of mercy and kindness will hear the prayers
  we now offer in the silence of our hearts
  [Pause . . .]:
  let us pray to the Lord.

Lord of all creation,
you have raised us to new life
through water and the Spirit.
May your Spirit of justice and peace
always rest upon us
so that we may dedicate ourselves
to the work of the prayers we have offered.
In Jesus' name, we pray.

Rend your hearts . . . and return to the Lord. Joel 2:12-18

Now is the day of salvation! 2 Corinthians 5:20–6:2

"Your Father who sees what is hidden will repay you." Matthew 6:1-6, 16-18

Now is the acceptable time!
The day of salvation has come!
With confident hope, then, let us pray:

- For our Church and parish community,
  that reconciliation with God and with one another
  will be the center of our Lenten observance:
  let us pray to the Lord.

- For the peoples and nations of the world,
  that they may become instruments of God's justice and peace:
  let us pray to the Lord.

- For those who will be preparing for baptism
  and for reception into the Church during this Lenten season,
  that these forty days may be a time of joyful discovery
  of God's great love for them:
  let us pray to the Lord.

- For families and households,
  that this Lent may be a time
  for renewing the bonds of love, trust, and acceptance:
  let us pray to the Lord.

- [For . . .,
  that . . .:
  let us pray to the Lord.]

- For the poor and the suffering,
  for the rejected and the forgotten,
  that our prayers and sacrifices this Lent
  may be the source of new hope and new beginnings for them:
  let us pray to the Lord.

- For those who have died in the peace of Christ
  [*especially* _____],
  that the joy of salvation may be theirs:
  let us pray to the Lord.

- For the prayers we now offer in the silence of our hearts
  [*Pause . . .*]:
  let us pray to the Lord.

Merciful God,
you bring us to life from the dust of the earth;
you re-create us in the waters of baptism;
you breathe into us the new life of the Risen Christ.
Look upon us as we enter these forty days,
bearing on our heads the mark of ashes.
May our fasting be a hunger for justice;
may our alms be the making of peace and reconciliation;
may our prayers be the hopes
    we are prepared to work and sacrifice for.
In Jesus' name, we pray.

The Lord God formed man . . . and blew into his nostrils the breath of life.

Genesis 2:7-9; 3:1-7

(The gift of Christ, the second Adam, brings life.) Romans 5:12-19

Jesus was led into the desert by the Spirit to be tempted by the devil. Matthew 4:1-11

In this Lenten springtime,
God calls us to be renewed in spirit.
Let us, therefore, open our hearts to God in prayer:

- That this Lent may be a time of reconciliation
  within our families, our parish, and our community:
  let us pray to the Lord.

- That those who serve our Church
  as pastors, teachers, and counselors
  may lead us in our search for the wisdom of God:
  let us pray to the Lord.

- That those who govern nations and human destinies
  may be committed to the justice and mercy of God,
  working unceasingly for the alleviation
  of hunger and misery in our world:
  let us pray to the Lord.

- That, in making moral and ethical choices,
  we may not bow before money, power, and prestige,
  but seek the wisdom and justice of God in all things:
  let us pray to the Lord.

- [That . . .:
  let us pray to the Lord.]

- That the God of mercy and compassion
  will be the refuge of the sick and the hope of the dying:
  let us pray to the Lord.

- That the faithful who have died
  [*especially* _____]
  may be reborn in the eternal life of the victorious Christ:
  let us pray to the Lord.

- That God our Father will hear the prayers
  we now offer in the silence of our hearts
  [Pause . . .]:
  let us pray to the Lord.

Hear the prayers we offer you, O Lord.
During these holy days of Lent,
may we dedicate ourselves to the work
of making these prayers a reality.
We ask these things of you
in the name of Jesus, our Redeemer.

(God's promise to Abram) "All the communities of the earth shall find blessing in you."
Genesis 12:1-4

God has saved us . . . not because of any merit of ours but according to his own design.
2 Timothy 1:8-10

[Jesus'] face became as dazzling as the sun, his clothes as radiant as light.
Matthew 17:1-9

Peter exclaimed on the mountain,
"Lord, how good that we are here!"
Confident of Christ's presence among us in this assembly,
let us pray for his gifts of healing and transformation:

- For our Church and parish community,
  that in our prayer and work together
  we may be a "blessing" to the world:
  let us pray to the Lord.

- For Pope N., Bishop N., Father N.,
  and all who serve the Church as pastors and teachers,
  that they may guide us into "clear light through the gospel":
  let us pray to the Lord.

- For the nations and peoples of the world,
  that they may become "great"
  in the justice and peace of God:
  let us pray to the Lord.

- For those experiencing loss or crisis in their lives,
  that, with our compassionate support and kindness,
  they may transform their heartache into joy,
  their despair into hope:
  let us pray to the Lord.

- For those who are preparing
  for baptism and reception into the Church,
  that their hearts may be opened
  to the Word of God's "beloved Son":
  let us pray to the Lord.

- [For . . .,
    that . . .:
    let us pray to the Lord.]

- For those who have died in Christ's peace
    [especially _____ *],*
    that they may be saved through the grace of Jesus our Savior:
    let us pray to the Lord.

- For the prayers we now make in the silence of our hearts
    [Pause . . .]:
    let us pray to the Lord.

Father, hear the prayers we bring before you.
May your Spirit of love and peace
transfigure us and our world
into the image of Jesus, the Risen Christ,
in whose name we offer these prayers.

(God tells Moses at Horeb,) "Strike the rock, and the water will flow from it for the people to drink." Exodus 17:3-7

[Christ] our hope will not leave us disappointed. Romans 5:1-2, 5-8

(Jesus meets the Samaritan woman at Jacob's well.) John 4:5-42

Christ is our peace and hope—
a hope that "will not leave us disappointed."
With confidence, then, let us pray:

- That this Lenten season may be a time of reconciliation
  within our families and our Church and parish:
  let us pray to the Lord.

- That our city [town], state, and nation
  may seek to share the wellsprings of our land
  with the poor and struggling countries of the world:
  let us pray to the Lord.

- That the Churches and communities of the Christian world
  may look beyond their different expressions of faith
  and worship God together "in Spirit and truth":
  let us pray to the Lord.

- That the divorced and separated
  and couples experiencing difficult times in their marriages
  may realize anew the presence of Christ in their midst:
  let us pray to the Lord.

- [That . . .:
  let us pray to the Lord.]

- That those who thirst for justice,
  for compassion and love,
  for health and happiness,
  may drink from Christ, the fountain of life:
  let us pray to the Lord.

- That those who have died
  [especially _____ *]*
  and those who will return to God during this Lenten season
  may experience the eternal life of the victorious Christ:
  let us pray to the Lord.

- That God will hear the prayers
  we now offer in the silence of our hearts
  [Pause . . .]:
  let us pray to the Lord.

We come before you, O Lord,
with open and humble hearts.
Give us the vision to seek you in all things,
that our lives may be made complete in your joy
and made whole in your compassionate love.
Hear these prayers which we ask of you
in the name of Jesus, our Savior.

(The Lord raises up the young David of Bethlehem as king.) 2 Samuel 16:1, 6-7, 10-13

You are light in the Lord. Ephesians 5:8-14

(The healing of the man born blind) John 9:1-41

Let us pray that God's light may illuminate
the minds and hearts of all people:

- For our Church and parish community,
  that we may share the vision
  of gospel compassion and mercy in our life together:
  let us pray to the Lord.

- For our bishops, priests, ministers, and religious educators,
  that God's work may show forth
  in their ministry among us:
  let us pray to the Lord.

- For those who develop and govern matters of public policy,
  that the dignity and sacredness of every person
  may be upheld and honored:
  let us pray to the Lord.

- For those who provide medical and pastoral care,
  that they may open our eyes
  to the wonders of God's love for us
  in all of life and creation:
  let us pray to the Lord.

- [For . . .,
  that . . .:
  let us pray to the Lord.]

- For those who are mentally impaired or physically disabled,
  that we may be given the grace and wisdom
  to enable them to use their gifts
  for the benefit of the entire human family:
  let us pray to the Lord.

- For those who have died
  [especially _____ *],*
  that they may one day awake and arise in the light of Christ:
  let us pray to the Lord.

- For the prayers we now offer in the silence of our hearts
  [Pause . . .]:
  let us pray to the Lord.

Lord of light,
grant us your vision of selfless love
that we may make real in our lives
the prayers and hopes
that you alone see in the depths of our hearts.
Hear the prayers which we ask of you
in the name of Jesus, the healing Christ.

I will open your graves and have you rise from them.	Ezekiel 37:12-14
The Spirit of God dwells in you.	Romans 8:8-11
(Jesus raises Lazarus from the dead.)	John 11:1-45

With the faith and hope of Martha, let us call upon the Lord in prayer:

- That the Spirit of God may dwell in every dimension
  of our life together as a Church and parish community:
  let us pray to the Lord.

- That all who serve the Church
  as bishops, priests, preachers, and teachers
  may be ministers of healing and compassion:
  let us pray to the Lord.

- That the public policies and laws
  of our city [town], state, and nation
  may protect the defenseless
  and provide for the poor and destitute
  with compassion and dignity:
  let us pray to the Lord.

- That those who are entombed
  by illness, substance abuse, violence, or fear
  may be raised up to a new life of hope and fulfillment:
  let us pray to the Lord.

- That those who grieve and mourn,
  and those who are coping with shattered relationships,
  may experience God's presence
  in our loving care and support of them:
  let us pray to the Lord.

- [That . . .:
  let us pray to the Lord.]

- That those who have gone before us
  marked with the sign of faith
  [especially _____ *]*
  may find light, happiness, and peace
  in the presence of the Risen Christ:
  let us pray to the Lord.

- That God will hear the prayers
  we now offer in the silence of our hearts
  [Pause . . .]:
  let us pray to the Lord.

Christ our Redeemer, you cried for your friend Lazarus:
cry for us and with us in our confusion and despair.
Risen Lord, you raised your friend from the tomb:
raise us up from the tombs of sin and death
to your life of understanding and hope.
Hear the prayers we offer to you,
who lives and reigns with the Father and the Holy Spirit
as the one God,
for ever and ever.

I gave my back to those who beat me.   Isaiah 50:4-7

[Christ] emptied himself . . . obediently accepting even death.   Philippians 2:6-11

(The Passion of Our Lord Jesus Christ)   YEAR A: Matthew 26:14–27:66
                                                 YEAR B: Mark 14:1–15:47
                                                 YEAR C: Luke 22:14–23:56

Let us now join our hearts and voices
in prayer to God our Father,
in the name of Jesus, the humble and obedient Servant of God:

- That our Church and parish community may proclaim
  humanity's liberation from sin by the cross of Christ:
  let us pray to the Lord.

- That those who serve our Church
  as pastors, counselors, and teachers
  may speak God's comforting, healing word
  to all the holy people of God:
  let us pray to the Lord.

- That the nations and governments of the world
  may be dedicated to the cause of Christ's peace and peace:
  let us pray to the Lord.

- That the sick, the suffering, the alienated, and the dying
  may know the healing presence of Christ:
  let us pray to the Lord.

- That we may imitate the attitude
  of the humble and obedient Jesus
  by emptying ourselves for the sake of the poor,
  the hungry, the homeless, and the forgotten:
  let us pray to the Lord.

- [That . . .:
  let us pray to the Lord.]

- That those who have died in the peace of Christ
  [especially _____]
  may share in the victory of his resurrection:
  let us pray to the Lord.

- That the God of mercy will hear the prayers we now offer
  in the silence of our hearts
  [Pause . . .]:
  let us pray to the Lord.

Father of endless love and compassion,
hear the prayers of your family gathered around your altar.
May we imitate your Son
by taking up our crosses with joyful obedience,
    seeking your justice in all things;
may we embrace his example of loving humility,
    loving and praising you
    in the compassion and care we extend to one another.
We ask these things in the name of your Son,
Jesus Christ, our Lord and Redeemer.

(The Passover of the Lord) Exodus 12:1-8, 11-14

Every time . . . you eat this bread and drink this cup, you proclaim the death of the Lord until he comes! 1 Corinthians 11:23-26

"If I washed your feet—I who am Teacher and Lord—then you must wash each other's feet." John 13:1-15

In the name of Jesus,
our salvation, life, and resurrection,
let us offer our prayers to God:

- For our Church and parish
  and for all the people of God,
  that we may follow the example of Christ,
  who washed the feet of his disciples:
  let us pray to the Lord.

- For Pope N., Bishop N., Father N.,
  and for all bishops, priests, and deacons,
  that they may be faithful imitators of Christ the Servant:
  let us pray to the Lord.

- For the nations and peoples of the world,
  that Christ's peace and justice may reign forever:
  let us pray to the Lord.

- For those who teach the gospel,
  that they may bring the life of Christ to young and old alike:
  let us pray to the Lord.

- For those who serve the poor, the homeless, and the dying,
  that God will bless their work with joy:
  let us pray to the Lord.

- For the sick and dying,
  that the peace and healing of the Risen Christ may be theirs:
  let us pray to the Lord.

- For the suffering and imprisoned,
  for the addicted and the abused,
  that they may know the freedom of the cross:
  let us pray to the Lord.

- For our deceased brothers and sisters,
  that they may live forever in the light of the Risen Christ:
  let us pray to the Lord.

- For the prayers we offer in the silence of our hearts
  [Pause . . .]:
  let us pray to the Lord.

Father in heaven, hear the prayers we make before you.
May we serve you by serving one another;
may we give you thanks for Christ, our Passover bread,
    by becoming bread for one another;
may we rejoice in these Easter mysteries
    by becoming light and healing for our broken world.
We offer these prayers through Christ, our Lord and Redeemer.

"Do not be afraid! Go and carry the news to my brothers that they are to go to Galilee, where they will see me." YEAR A: Matthew 28:1-10

"You are looking for Jesus of Nazareth, the one who was crucified. He has been raised up; he is not here." YEAR B: Mark 16:1-8

"Why do you search for the living One among the dead? He is not here; he has been raised up." YEAR C: Luke 24:1-12

On this most holy night [morning]
let us pray with one mind and heart
that the joy of Easter may be shared by all the world:

- For our Church and parish family,
  that we may become a community of the Resurrection:
  let us pray to the Lord.

- For Pope N., Bishop N., Father N.,
  and for all who serve the Church,
  that they may proclaim the good news of the empty tomb:
  let us pray to the Lord.

- For the nations and peoples of the world,
  that the peace of the Risen Christ may reign forever:
  let us pray to the Lord.

- For all who are baptized
  and welcomed into our Church this night [morning],
  that they may die to sin
  and rise to the new life of the Risen Christ:
  let us pray to the Lord.

- For all who serve the poor, the homeless, and the dying,
  that God will bless their work with joy:
  let us pray to the Lord.

- For the sick and dying,
  for the suffering and the imprisoned,
  for the addicted and the abused,
  that they may be freed from their infirmities
  and re-created in the life of the Risen Christ:
  let us pray to the Lord.

- For our deceased brothers and sisters,
  that they may rise to the new life of the victorious Christ:
  let us pray to the Lord.

- For the prayers we offer in the silence of our hearts
  [Pause . . .]:
  let us pray to the Lord.

Father of life, Author of love,
in raising your Son from the grave
all of creation has been reborn.
May the life and love of the paschal mystery
that we celebrate tonight [this morning]
be a constant and lasting reality in our lives.
We ask this through Christ, our Risen Lord.

(Peter's testimony) "They killed [Jesus] finally, 'hanging him on a tree,'
only to have God raise him up on the third day." Acts 10:34, 37-43

Get rid of the old yeast to make of yourselves fresh dough. 1 Corinthians 5:6-8

Peter . . . observed the wrappings on the ground and saw the piece of cloth which had
covered the head . . . rolled up in a place by itself. John 20:1-9

In the Easter mystery,
God has re-created our world
in joy, peace, hope, and light.
And so we pray:

- That the *joy* of the Risen Christ
  may inspire our parish community to proclaim,
  in our work and worship together,
  the good news of the empty tomb:
  let us pray to the Lord.

- That the *peace* of the Risen Christ
  reign among the nations and peoples of the world,
  leading them to work together to uphold
  the sacred dignity of all men, women, and children:
  let us pray to the Lord.

- That the *hope* of the Risen Christ
  may console the troubled,
  reconcile those who are estranged and alienated,
  and heal the hurting and suffering among us:
  let us pray to the Lord.

- That the *light* of the Risen Christ
  may shine on the souls
  of all our deceased relatives and friends
  [especially _____]:
  let us pray to the Lord.

- That the Father, who raised Jesus from the grave,
  will grant the prayers
  we now make in the silence of our hearts
  [Pause . . .]:
  let us pray to the Lord.

Father of life, Author of love,
in raising your Son from the grave
all of creation has been reborn.
May the life and love of the Paschal mystery,
which we celebrate today,
be a constant and lasting reality in our lives.
We ask this through Christ, our Risen Lord.

The brethren devoted themselves to the apostles' instruction and the communal life,
to the breaking of bread and the prayers.   Acts 2:42-47

Praised be the God . . . who in his great mercy, gave us a new birth . . . which
draws its life from the resurrection of Jesus Christ from the dead.   1 Peter 1:3-9

[Jesus said] to Thomas: "Do not persist in your unbelief, but believe!"   John 20:19-31

In peace
let us join our hearts and voices in prayer to the Lord:

- For our Church and parish,
  that we may be a community united in faith,
  prayer, and the "breaking of bread":
  let us pray to the Lord.

- For Pope N., Bishop N., Father N.,
  and for all who lead and serve our Church,
  that they may be ministers of forgiveness
  and prophets of peace:
  let us pray to the Lord.

- For all Christian Churches and communities,
  that they may accomplish great things
  through the faith we share in Jesus, the Risen One:
  let us pray to the Lord.

- For all nations and peoples,
  that the gift of Christ's peace may be theirs:
  let us pray to the Lord.

- [For . . .,
  that . . .:
  let us pray to the Lord.]

- For the poor and the needy,
  for the forgotten and lost,
  that we may reach out to them,
  not from our surplus,
  but from our treasure:
  let us pray to the Lord.

- For the faithful who have died
  [*especially* _____],
  that they may have life in the name of the Risen Christ:
  let us pray to the Lord.

- For the prayers we now make in the silence of our hearts
  [*Pause . . .*]:
  let us pray to the Lord.

Grant us, O Lord, your peace:
the peace that enables us to constantly discover your joy;
the peace that impels us to seek your justice in all things;
the peace that allows us to suffer for what is right and good;
the peace that invites us to call
    every man, woman, and child "friend."
Hear the prayers we offer for peace—
the peace of Jesus Christ, our Lord and Risen Savior,
who lives and reigns with you and the Holy Spirit
for ever and ever.

(Peter's Pentecost sermon) "God freed [Jesus] from death's bitter pangs . . .
and raised him up again." Acts 2:14, 22-28

Conduct yourselves reverently during your sojourn in a strange land. 1 Peter 1:17-21

(The two disciples recognized Jesus in the breaking of bread.) Luke 24:13-35

In the name of Jesus, the Risen One,
let us offer our prayers to God:

- That, in the breaking of the bread,
  we may recognize the love and mercy of God for all of us:
  let us pray to the Lord.

- That Pope N., Bishop N., Father N.,
  and all priests, deacons, and ministers
  may proclaim, with courage and conviction,
  the good news of Christ's resurrection:
  let us pray to the Lord.

- That all the world's peoples, nations, and communities
  may celebrate that peace
  which shatters boundaries and divisions:
  let us pray to the Lord.

- That neither work nor the values of the marketplace
  may displace God as the center of our faith and hope:
  let us pray to the Lord.

- [That . . .:
  let us pray to the Lord.]

- That all "who sojourn in a strange land"
  of poverty and oppression
  may find help and hope
  in our compassionate response to their plight:
  let us pray to the Lord.

- That those who have died in the peace of Christ
  [especially _____]
  may rejoice in his presence forever:
  let us pray to the Lord.

- That the God of mercy and love will hear the prayers
  we now make in the silence of our hearts
  [Pause . . .]:
  let us pray to the Lord.

May the prayers we make with one voice, O Lord,
make us one in heart and mind, as well.
May the joy of this Easter season
impel us to share that joy
with those whose lives have not yet been touched
by the new life of the Risen One,
who lives and reigns with you for ever and ever.

(Peter's Pentecost sermon) "It was to you and your children that the promise was made, and to all those still far off whom the Lord our God calls." Acts 2:14, 36-41

By [Christ's] wounds you were healed. 1 Peter 2:20-25

"I am the sheepgate. . . . I came that they might have life and have it to the full." John 10:1-10

Let us join our hearts and voices in prayer to the Lord,
our Father and Shepherd:

- For our parish community,
  that together we may live the gospel of the Good Shepherd
  in a spirit of peace and concern for one another:
  let us pray to the Lord.

- For our bishops and priests, pastors and teachers,
  that they may lead the Church to God
  through Christ the "sheepgate":
  let us pray to the Lord.

- For all who govern and conduct the affairs of nations,
  that they may enact laws and public policies
  which uphold the sacred dignity of every person
  as a child of God:
  let us pray to the Lord.

- For those who speak for the persecuted
  and who suffer with the oppressed,
  that Christ, who gives his life for his sheep,
  may be their power and strength:
  let us pray to the Lord.

- [For . . .,
  that . . .:
  let us pray to the Lord.]

- For the sick, the suffering, the recovering, and the dying,
  that, by Christ's sufferings, they may be healed:
  let us pray to the Lord.

- For our deceased relatives and friends
  [especially _____],
  that they may dwell forever in the house of God:
  let us pray to the Lord.

- For the prayers we now make in the silence of our hearts
  [Pause . . .]:
  let us pray to the Lord.

Father of love and Lord of life,
hear our Easter prayers.
Give us the vision of faith and the courage of hope
to embrace the life of the Risen Christ,
''and have it to the full.''
We ask this in the name of your Son, our Lord Jesus Christ,
who lives and reigns with you and the Holy Spirit
as the one God
for ever and ever.

The Twelve . . . prayed over [the seven deacons] and then imposed hands on them.

Acts 6:1-7

You . . . are living stones, built as an edifice of spirit.　　　1 Peter 2:4-9

"In my Father's house there are many dwelling places."　　　John 14:1-12

Confident that our faith in God will never disappoint us,
let us make our prayers known to the Father in Jesus' name:

- For our parish community,
  that, in our ministries of prayer and charity,
  we may always accomplish the work of God:
  let us pray to the Lord.

- For the bishops, priests, and deacons of our Church,
  that they may be dedicated to prayer
  and the ministry of the Word:
  let us pray to the Lord.

- For all Christian Churches and communities,
  that these "living stones"
  may come together as an "edifice of spirit":
  let us pray to the Lord.

- For those who have dedicated their lives
  to the service of others,
  that their selflessness may reveal to all
  the depth of God's love:
  let us pray to the Lord.

- [For . . .,
  that . . .:
  let us pray to the Lord.]

- For those who are overcome by grief, despair, or bitterness,
  for those who are trapped in lives of poverty or pain,
  that Christ may lead them
  "from darkness into his marvelous light":
  let us pray to the Lord.

- For all who have died in the peace of Christ
  [especially _____],
  that they may dwell in the places
  prepared for them by the Risen One:
  let us pray to the Lord.

- For the prayers we now offer in the silence of our hearts
  [Pause . . .]:
  let us pray to the Lord.

Hear our Easter prayers, O Lord.
May the darkness of despair and anguish in our lives
be forever shattered by your ''marvelous light'' of Easter joy.
We ask this in the name of your Son, our Lord Jesus Christ,
who lives and reigns with you and the Holy Spirit
as the one God
for ever and ever.

Philip went down to the town of Samaria and there proclaimed the Messiah.

Acts 8:5-8, 14-17

Christ died for sins once for all . . . so that he could lead you to God. 1 Peter 3:15-18

"The Spirit of truth . . . will be within you." John 14:15-21

The Risen Lord is present in our midst.
In joyful hope, then, let us pray:

- That the Spirit of truth may dwell always
  in the midst of our Church and parish community:
  let us pray to the Lord.

- That those who serve our Church
  as bishops, priests, deacons, and ministers
  may reveal the love of God
  in their humble and dedicated service to God's people:
  let us pray to the Lord.

- That the nations and peoples of the earth
  may recognize and accept the Paraclete of justice and peace:
  let us pray to the Lord.

- That families experiencing pain and difficult times
  may rediscover God's Spirit of love in their midst:
  let us pray to the Lord.

- [That . . .:
  let us pray to the Lord.]

- That the sick, the suffering, and the troubled
  may rejoice in the healing presence of Christ:
  let us pray to the Lord.

- That the Risen Christ will gather before the Father
  the souls of all the faithful who have died
  [especially _____]:
  let us pray to the Lord.

- That the God of mercy will hear the prayers
  we now offer in the silence of our hearts
  [Pause . . .]:
  let us pray to the Lord.

In times of darkness and turmoil,
in times when we feel lost and abandoned,
make your presence known to us, O Risen Savior,
that we may bring your love and truth to our hurting world.
Hear these prayers we ask of you,
who lives and reigns with the Father and the Holy Spirit
as the one God
for ever and ever.

[Jesus] was lifted up before [the apostles'] eyes in a cloud which took him from their sight.
Acts 1:1-11

[The Father] has put all things under Christ's feet and has made him thus exalted,
head of the church, which is his body. Ephesians 1:17-23

(Jesus returns to the Father.) YEAR A: Matthew 28:16-20
YEAR B: Mark 16:15-20
YEAR C: Luke 24:46-53

The Risen Christ now sits at God's right hand
until the end of time.
In confidence and hope, then,
let us offer our prayers:

- That our Church and parish family
  may be witnesses of the Risen Christ
  in our own community and to the ends of the earth:
  let us pray to the Lord.

- That the bishops, priests, deacons, and ministers of our Church
  may continue the great mission
  entrusted by Christ to the Eleven:
  let us pray to the Lord.

- That every nation, power, and dominion of the earth
  may give praise to God through their work together
  for justice and peace for all peoples:
  let us pray to the Lord.

- That all who seek to be disciples of Jesus may receive
  "a spirit of wisdom and insight to know [God] clearly":
  let us pray to the Lord.

- [That . . .:
  let us pray to the Lord.]

- That the poor, the sick, the suffering, and the needy
  may come to know, in our outreach to them,
  "the great hope" to which God has called us all:
  let us pray to the Lord.

- That our deceased relatives and friends
  [especially _____]
  may be reborn in the life of the Risen Christ:
  let us pray to the Lord.

- That God, our loving Father, will hear the prayers
  we now make in the silence our hearts
  [Pause . . .]:
  let us pray to the Lord.

Father, in raising the Lord Jesus from the grave
you have given hope to us and to all humanity.
Hear the prayers we make to you
in the name of Jesus the Christ,
the source and life of that hope,
who lives and reigns with you
for ever and ever.

The apostles returned to Jerusalem.   Acts 1:12-14

Happy are you when you are insulted for the sake of Christ.   1 Peter 4:13-16

(Jesus prayed) "I entrusted to [these] the message you entrusted to me."

       John 17:1-11

Let us now join our prayers
to Christ's eternal prayer to God for all the human family:

- For our Church and parish,
  that we may become a community of prayer
  and loving support to one another:
  let us pray to the Lord.

- For those to be ordained to the priesthood and diaconate,
  for seminarians, postulants, and novices,
  and for those preparing for lives of service,
  that they will find joy and fulfillment in their ministries:
  let us pray to the Lord.

- For teachers of religious education,
  for those who bring others to the joy of faith,
  that they may share the message
  which God entrusted to Christ
  and Christ has entrusted to his Church:
  let us pray to the Lord.

- For students, especially those graduating this spring,
  that their studies may lead them
  not only to competence and knowledge
  but to the wisdom and love of God:
  let us pray to the Lord.

- For those who continue to make known the love of God
  in the midst of persecution and ridicule,
  that their brave and constant witness will, one day,
  be their glory:
  let us pray to the Lord.

- [For . . .,
  that . . .:
  let us pray to the Lord.]

- For the faithful who have died
  [especially _____ *]*,
  that they may dwell in the house of God forever:
  let us pray to the Lord.

- For the prayers we now offer in the silence of our hearts
  [Pause . . .]:
  let us pray to the Lord.

Gracious God, hear the prayers of the people
gathered together by your Son.
May every prayer we utter and every work we undertake
be to your glory
as we await the fulfillment of your Easter promise
of eternal life in you
and he whom you have sent, Jesus Christ,
who lives and reigns with you for ever and ever.

They began to express themselves in foreign tongues and make bold proclamation
as the Spirit prompted them. Acts 2:1-11

To each person the manifestation of the Spirit is given for the common good.
1 Corinthians 12:3-7, 12-13

"Receive the Holy Spirit. If you forgive men's sins, they are forgiven them."
John 20:19-23

Gathered in this place,
we have come to celebrate God's Spirit dwelling among us.
Let us give voice to that Spirit
in the prayers we offer together:

- That the Spirit of God may inspire us
  to joyfully use our gifts and talents
  for the common good of the one body of Christ:
  let us pray to the Lord.

- That our bishops, priests, deacons, and ministers
  may boldly proclaim the joy and hope of the Resurrection:
  let us pray to the Lord.

- That all the peoples of the earth
  may hear the good news of the "marvels God has accomplished":
  let us pray to the Lord.

- That the Spirit of God will make each one of us
  a minister of peace and forgiveness
  in our homes, schools, and workplaces:
  let us pray to the Lord.

- [That . . .:
  let us pray to the Lord.]

- That those who are alienated from loved ones,
  who are bitter, afraid, and without hope,
  may rediscover God's breath of life within them:
  let us pray to the Lord.

- That our deceased relatives and friends
  [especially _____ *]*
  may rest forever in the eternal peace of Christ:
  let us pray to the Lord.

- That God will hear the prayers we now make
  in the silence of our hearts
  [Pause . . .]:
  let us pray to the Lord.

Father of life, hear our prayers.
Re-create us in your Holy Spirit
so that we may be a source of forgiveness
and a community of hope
for our hurting world.
We make this prayer in the name of Jesus, the Risen Christ,
who lives and reigns with you and the Holy Spirit
as the one God
for ever and ever.

The Lord stood with Moses there and proclaimed his name, "Lord." Exodus 34:4-6, 8-9

The grace of the Lord Jesus Christ, and the love of God, and the fellowship of the Holy Spirit be with you all!   2 Corinthians 13:11-13

"God so loved the world that he gave his only Son . . . that the world might be saved through him."   John 3:16-18

To the merciful and gracious Lord of all, let us pray:

- For our Church and parish community,
  that, guided by the Spirit of God,
  we may not harbor judgment and condemnation,
  but seek instead reconciliation and peace:
  let us pray to the Lord.

- For those who serve the Church as pastors and ministers,
  that they may proclaim the great love of God—
  the love revealed to us by Christ Jesus
  and now present among us in the Holy Spirit:
  let us pray to the Lord.

- For the nations and peoples of the world,
  that they may recognize the sacredness of God's creation
  and work together for its just use and protection:
  let us pray to the Lord.

- For parents, teachers, and all who are entrusted
  with the care and education of children,
  that they may help our sons and daughters grow
  in God's ways of compassion and peace:
  let us pray to the Lord.

- [For . . .,
  that . . .:
  let us pray to the Lord.]

- For the sick, the suffering, and the dying,
  that they may live in the hope of the Risen Christ:
  let us pray to the Lord.

- For all our deceased relatives and friends
  [especially _____],
  that they may be heirs of the eternal life of God:
  let us pray to the Lord.

- For the prayers we now offer in the silence of our hearts
  [Pause . . .]:
  let us pray to the Lord.

Gracious God, we call out to you,
not as a mysterious, cosmic riddle,
but as you have made yourself known to us:
    the God of compassion and love,
    the God who redeems us and restores us to life,
    the God who lives in us and through us.
Help us to love others as you love us,
without condition, without limit.
We make these prayers to you,
the Father, Son, and Spirit,
who lives and reigns for ever and ever.

Moses said to the people: ". . . not by bread alone does man live, but by every word that comes forth from the mouth of the Lord."   Deuteronomy 8:2-3, 14-16

Is not the bread we break a sharing in the body of Christ?   1 Corinthians 10:16-17

"I myself am the living bread come down from heaven."   John 6:51-58

God invites us to this table
to share the body and blood of Jesus in the Eucharist.
Let us raise our hearts and voices in prayer that,
through the Eucharist we are about to celebrate,
we might become eucharist for others:

- That we may be bread for one another—
  a parish community of support and compassion:
  let us pray to the Lord.

- That we may be bread for our world,
  proclaiming with courage and conviction
  the gospel of justice, mercy, and peace:
  let us pray to the Lord.

- That we may be bread for our children,
  teaching them the many wonderful things
  that God has done for us:
  let us pray to the Lord.

- That we may be bread for the poor and hungry,
  willingly sharing with them
  from the bounty we have been given:
  let us pray to the Lord.

- That we may be bread for all in need,
  welcoming all who come to our table
  seeking support, compassion, and understanding:
  let us pray to the Lord.

- [That we may be bread for . . .:
  let us pray to the Lord.]

- That all our deceased relatives and friends
  [especially _____ *]*
  may feast on the Bread of Life forever
  at God's heavenly table:
  let us pray to the Lord.

- That we may be bread for all in need
  through the prayers we now offer
  in the silence of our hearts
  [Pause . . .]:
  let us pray to the Lord.

Gracious Father, Giver and Nurturer of all life,
hear our prayers.
May the bread and wine of the Eucharist
make us bread for one another and for all,
that we might become ministers of your life and love
to our hurting world.
We ask this in the name of Jesus, the Bread of Life.

I will make you a light to the nations, that my salvation may reach to the ends of the earth.   Isaiah 49:3, 5-6

[You have been called to be a holy people.]   1 Corinthians 1:1-3

"Look there! The Lamb of God who takes away the sin of the world!"   John 1:29-34

In baptism God has made us a consecrated people,
a people called to holiness.
In this spirit, then, let us pray:

- That, as a parish community,
  we may give witness to the presence of the Lamb of God
  in our community and our world:
  let us pray to the Lord.

- That the good news of Christ Jesus
  taught by our bishops, priests, deacons, and ministers
  "may reach to the ends of the earth":
  let us pray to the Lord.

- That our nation may recommit itself
  to the principles of liberty and justice
  for all men, women, and children,
  regardless of race, nationality, or creed:
  let us pray to the Lord.

- [That . . .:
  let us pray to the Lord.]

- That families in crisis and communities in turmoil
  may find hope and healing
  in God's Spirit of reconciliation and forgiveness:
  let us pray to the Lord.

- That we may recognize the Spirit of God
  in the work and sacrifice
  of those who work with the poor,
  the oppressed, and the forgotten:
  let us pray to the Lord.

- That the light of God's mercy and peace
  will shine upon the deceased members
  of our families and parish
  [especially _____]:
  let us pray to the Lord.

- That God will hear the prayers we now make
  in the silence of our hearts
  [Pause . . .]:
  let us pray to the Lord.

Hear the prayers of your people, O God.
May your Spirit rest upon each one of us
that we may create our lives and our world anew
in your love and mercy.
We ask this in the name of Jesus, the Christ.

The people who walked in darkness have seen a great light. Isaiah 8:23–9:3

Let there be no factions; rather, be united in mind and judgment.
1 Corinthians 1:10-13, 17

"Come after me and I will make you fishers of [souls]." Matthew 4:12-23

Jesus Christ, the great Light of God,
has dawned upon our world.
In joyful hope, then, let us pray:

- That the gospel of Christ
  may be the center of our life together
  as a Church and parish community:
  let us pray to the Lord.

- That Pope N., Bishop N., Father N.,
  and the bishops, priests, deacons, and ministers of our Church
  may be compassionate "fishers" of souls for God:
  let us pray to the Lord.

- That all Churches and faith communities
  may find unity in the gospel of the Risen Christ:
  let us pray to the Lord.

- That the nations and peoples of the world may live in peace,
  working together to protect the dignity and rights
  of every member of the human family:
  let us pray to the Lord.

- [That . . .:
  let us pray to the Lord.]

- That those who walk in the darkness
  of illness, addiction, and abuse
  may see the "great light" of Christ:
  let us pray to the Lord.

- That the faithful who have died
  [especially _____ *]*
  may "dwell forever in the house of the Lord":
  let us pray to the Lord.

- That our Father in heaven will hear the prayers
  we now make in the silence of our hearts
  [Pause . . .]:
  let us pray to the Lord.

Lord of light, dispel the darkness
of our self-centeredness and ignorance.
May these prayers we offer together
be the first light of your presence
in our homes and communities.
We offer these prayers to you, O God,
in the name of your Son, our Lord Jesus Christ.

I will leave as a remnant in your midst a people humble and lowly.

Zephaniah 2:3; 3:12-13

God chose those whom the world considers absurd to shame the wise.

1 Corinthians 1:26-31

"How blest are the poor in spirit: the reign of God is theirs."   Matthew 5:1-12

Let us join our hearts and voices in prayer to the Lord:

- For our Church and parish community,
  that we may always be the faithful "remnant"
  of the Lord's peace and justice:
  let us pray to the Lord.

- For Pope N., Bishop N., Father N.,
  and for all who serve the Church as pastors and teachers,
  that they may proclaim the reign of God
  to our broken world:
  let us pray to the Lord.

- For religious communities of men and women,
  for all who live vowed lives
  of poverty, chastity, and obedience,
  that their single-hearted search for God
  may lead others to the joy of God's kingdom:
  let us pray to the Lord.

- For the nations and peoples of the world,
  that they may dedicate themselves
  to the work of peacemaking:
  let us pray to the Lord.

- [For . . .,
  that . . .:
  let us pray to the Lord.]

- For the poor and suffering,
  the abandoned and forgotten,
  and for those who serve them,
  that their humble witness to God's love
  will shame those who victimize them:
  let us pray to the Lord.

- For those who have died
  [especially _____],
  that they may inherit the reward of heaven awaiting them:
  let us pray to the Lord.

- For the prayers we now make in the silence of our hearts
  [Pause . . .]:
  let us pray to the Lord.

Hear our prayers for the needs of all people, O Lord.
Give us your grace and vision
that we might become a people of the Beatitudes—
a people who seek your presence and joy in all things.
In Jesus' name, we pray.

If you bestow your bread on the hungry . . . then light shall rise for you
in the darkness. Isaiah 58:7-10

Your faith rests not on the wisdom of men but on the power of God.

1 Corinthians 2:1-5

"You are the salt of the earth . . . the light of the world." Matthew 5:13-16

Let us now pray that the light of God
may dawn upon all God's holy people:

- That we may be the "salt of the earth,"
  bringing the compassion and peace of God
  to our homes and communities:
  let us pray to the Lord.

- That our Church may be a "light" for the world,
  reflecting in our worship and ministries
  the love and forgiveness of God:
  let us pray to the Lord.

- That all nations, states, and cities
  may seek the justice of God for all people:
  let us pray to the Lord.

- [That . . .:
  let us pray to the Lord.]

- That our compassionate God may be present to us
  in times of pain, despair, and grief:
  let us pray to the Lord.

- That the poor, the hungry, and the oppressed
  may always find a place of warmth and welcome among us:
  let us pray to the Lord.

- That those who have died
  [especially _____]
  may walk forever in the light of the Risen Christ:
  let us pray to the Lord.

- That God will hear the prayers
  we now make in the silence of our hearts
  [Pause . . .]:
  let us pray to the Lord.

Lord God, we cry to you for help.
May the good we do for others,
the compassion we offer to those in need,
and the justice we seek for all men and women
make us worthy of your favorable hearing of these prayers.
In Jesus' name, we pray.

There are set before you fire and water, . . . life and death . . . . Sirach 15:15-20

What we utter is God's wisdom: a mysterious, a hidden wisdom. 1 Corinthians 2:6-10

"I have come, not to abolish [the law and the prophets], but to fulfill them."
Matthew 5:17-37

Before offering our gifts at this altar,
let us unite our hearts in prayer for all the people of God:

- That our Church and parish community
  may seek the life and love of God in all things:
  let us pray to the Lord.

- That our bishops, priests, deacons,
  and all who serve the Church
  may be ministers of God's forgiveness and reconciliation:
  let us pray to the Lord.

- That the nations, governments, and peoples of the world
  may realize the goodness of all that God has made
  and work together for the just use of the earth's gifts:
  let us pray to the Lord.

- That students and young people
  may be inspired by God's holy wisdom
  to make responsible and mature decisions
  in the choices and challenges
  that will face them in their lives:
  let us pray to the Lord.

- [That . . .:
  let us pray to the Lord.]

- That the poor and the homeless,
  the sick and the suffering,
  the addicted and the abused,
  may find, among us, compassion and support:
  let us pray to the Lord.

- That God will welcome into the heavenly kingdom
  the souls of all who have died in God's peace
  [especially _____]:
  let us pray to the Lord.

- That God will hear the prayers
  we now make in the silence of our hearts
  [Pause . . .]:
  let us pray to the Lord.

To you, O God, nothing is hidden;
from you, O Lord, no secrets are kept.
Hear the prayers and hopes of our hearts
that we might have the courage
to speak what we hope for
and to live what we seek.
In Jesus' name, we pray.

"Be holy, for I, the Lord, your God, am holy." Leviticus 19:1-2, 17-18

You are the temple of God, . . . the Spirit of God dwells in you. 1 Corinthians 3:16-23

"You must be perfected as your heavenly Father is perfect." Matthew 5:38-48

The Lord God is present in the midst of this holy assembly.
Let us call to the Lord in prayer:

- For our Church and parish community,
  that the Spirit of God may dwell
  within our common life of prayer and works of charity:
  let us pray to the Lord.

- For Pope N., Bishop N., Father N.,
  and for all who serve the Church,
  that they may be prophets
  of the wisdom and compassion of God:
  let us pray to the Lord.

- For President N., Governor N., and for the leaders
  of the world's nations, states, and cities,
  that a realization of the holiness of every human person
  may guide their work for their people:
  let us pray to the Lord.

- For those who fight against racism,
  oppression, and social injustice,
  that their courageous witness may inspire all of us
  to work for justice and peace:
  let us pray to the Lord.

- [For . . .,
  that . . .:
  let us pray to the Lord.]

- For those from whom we are separated or alienated,
  for those who we have forgotten or ignored,
  that God will grant us the grace
  to take the first step toward reconciliation with them:
  let us pray to the Lord.

- For those who have died in the peace of Christ
  [*especially* _____],
  that the eternal life of God may be theirs:
  let us pray to the Lord.

- For the prayers we now make in the silence of our hearts
  [*Pause . . .*]:
  let us pray to the Lord.

Lord God, Father of us all,
hear the prayers we make to you
for every member of the human family.
Open our hearts to your Spirit
that we may seek an end to bitterness and discord,
so that we might become your holy people,
a community of light and peace.
We ask this through Christ our Lord.

Can a mother forget her infant, be without tenderness for the child of her womb?
Isaiah 49:14-15

[God] will bring to light what is hidden in darkness and manifest the intentions of hearts.
1 Corinthians 4:1-5

"Seek first . . . [God's] way of holiness, and all these things will be given you besides."
Matthew 6:24-34

Christ has assured us
of God's constant compassion and providence.
In joyful confidence, then, let us pray:

- That our Church and parish community
  may be a place of peace and compassion for all:
  let us pray to the Lord.

- That pastors and religious educators
  may be faithful teachers of God's "way of holiness":
  let us pray to the Lord.

- That legislatures, courts, and government agencies
  may work ceaselessly to uphold the dignity
  of every man, woman, and child:
  let us pray to the Lord.

- That businesses and financial concerns
  will use the resources of the earth justly and responsibly:
  let us pray to the Lord.

- That God will bless with wisdom and love
  those called to the vocation of parenthood:
  let us pray to the Lord.

- [That . . .:
  let us pray to the Lord.]

- That the Risen Christ will bring into his Father's presence
  the souls of those who have died in his peace
  [especially _____]:
  let us pray to the Lord.

- That God will hear the prayers we now make
  in the silence of our hearts
  [Pause . . .]:
  let us pray to the Lord.

Lord God, Giver of life, hear us.
May the humility and sincerity of our prayer
be a blessing for us.
Give us the grace to make you
the center of our lives—
that we may seek your presence,
your truth, and your love
in all things.
In Jesus' name, we pray.

Moses told the people, . . . "I set before you here, this day, a blessing and a curse."
Deuteronomy 11:18, 26-28

The justice of God has been manifested apart from the law. Romans 3:21-25, 28

"Anyone who hears my words but does not put them into practice is like the foolish man who built his house on sandy ground." Matthew 7:21-27

To the Lord of kindness and hope, let us pray:

- For our Church and parish community,
  that our life together may be built
  on the "rock" of God's wisdom and truth:
  let us pray to the Lord.

- For Pope N., Bishop N., Father N.,
  and all who serve our Church,
  that they may set before the world
  the "blessing" of God's love and mercy:
  let us pray to the Lord.

- For President N., Governor N.,
  and all government officials and legislators,
  that they may seek the justice of God
  in all laws and public policies:
  let us pray to the Lord.

- [For . . .,
  that . . .:
  let us pray to the Lord.]

- For those whose homes and lives have been shattered
  by disaster or catastrophe,
  that we may respond to their plight
  with compassion and generosity:
  let us pray to the Lord.

- For the sick, the suffering, the recovering, and the dying,
  that God will be their "rock" and shelter:
  let us pray to the Lord.

- For those who have died
  [especially _____],
  that Christ will welcome them into the kingdom of his Father:
  let us pray to the Lord.

- That God our Savior and Protector will hear the prayers
  we now offer in the silence of our hearts
  [Pause . . .]:
  let us pray to the Lord.

Gracious God,
you are the rock on which we build our lives,
our shelter from the storms that endanger us,
the fire that gives light and warmth to our hearts.
Hear the prayers we offer for ourselves
and for all your holy people,
prayers we make in the name of your Son,
our Lord Jesus Christ.

It is love that I desire, not sacrifice. Hosea 6:3-6

Abraham believed, hoping against hope, and so became the father of many nations.
Romans 4:18-25

Jesus . . . saw a man named Matthew at his post where taxes were collected.
He said to him, "Follow me." Matthew 9:9-13

With Abraham's confidence in God's providence
and Matthew's faith in God's mercy,
let us offer our prayers to the Lord:

- That we may follow Christ in every dimension
  of our life together as a Church and parish community:
  let us pray to the Lord.

- That the bishops, priests, and ministers of our Church
  may bring healing and forgiveness
  to all who seek God:
  let us pray to the Lord.

- That the peace of God may reign among the nations
  and peoples of the earth
  "from the rising of the sun to its setting":
  let us pray to the Lord.

- That monastic and religious communities
  may teach the world the certainty of God's mercy
  and the hope of God's love:
  let us pray to the Lord.

- [That . . .:
  let us pray to the Lord.]

- That those who seek to rebuild their lives
  in the wake of loss, illness, abuse, or addiction
  may be assured of our unlimited, unconditional support:
  let us pray to the Lord.

- That the souls of our deceased relatives and friends
  [especially _____]
  may be raised up
  to the new life of God's Risen Son:
  let us pray to the Lord.

- That God will hear the prayers we now offer
  in the silence of our hearts
  [Pause . . .]:
  let us pray to the Lord.

Gracious God,
we lift up our prayers before you,
with the hope of Abraham
that you will be with us always,
and with the faith of Matthew
that to follow your Son is to discover your will.
Grant these prayers we ask
in the name of your Son,
our Lord and Redeemer, Jesus Christ.

You shall be my special possession, dearer to me than all other people. Exodus 19:2-6

We . . . make God our boast through our Lord Jesus Christ, through whom we have now received reconciliation. Romans 5:6-11

"Go . . . after the lost sheep of the house of Israel. As you go, make this announcement: 'The reign of God is at hand!'" Matthew 9:36–10:8

To God, who has done great things for us, let us pray:

- For our Church and parish community,
  that, in our work and worship together,
  we may be faithful to our call
  to be God's holy people:
  let us pray to the Lord.

- For Pope N., Bishop N., and for all the bishops of our Church,
  that they may faithfully continue the mission
  entrusted first to the apostles by Christ:
  let us pray to the Lord.

- For preachers and religious educators,
  that they may inspire their hearers and students
  with the gift of faith they have received:
  let us pray to the Lord.

- [For . . .,
  that . . .:
  let us pray to the Lord.]

- For the lost, the forgotten, and the oppressed,
  that the reconciling love of Christ the Shepherd
  may give them direction and hope:
  let us pray to the Lord.

- For the sick, the recovering, and the dying,
  that, in the midst of their suffering,
  they may know the hope of Christ's healing presence:
  let us pray to the Lord.

- For those who have died in the peace of Christ
  [especially _____],
  that the kingdom of God may be theirs:
  let us pray to the Lord.

- For the prayers we now offer in the silence of our hearts
  [Pause . . .]:
  let us pray to the Lord.

Hear our prayers, O God,
as we struggle to be your holy people,
a community of faith.
Guide our steps and enlighten our vision
as we travel together
to proclaim your reign in our time and place.
We ask these things in the name of your Son,
our Lord and Teacher, Jesus Christ.

The Lord is with me, . . . my persecutors will stumble, they will not triumph.
                                                            Jeremiah 20:10-13

The grace of God and the gracious gift of . . . Jesus Christ abound for all.
                                                            Romans 5:12-15

"Not a single sparrow falls to the ground without your Father's consent."
                                                            Matthew 10:26-33

Let us now offer our prayers to the God of goodness
in the name of God's Son, our Risen Savior:

- For our Church and parish community,
  that every prayer and good work of ours
  may proclaim God's presence among us:
  let us pray to the Lord.

- For those who serve our Church
  as pastors, teachers, and preachers,
  that their revelation of God's light
  may shatter the darkness of fear, hatred, and oppression:
  let us pray to the Lord.

- For the nations and peoples of the world,
  that their common pursuit of justice and equality
  may destroy racism, poverty, and persecution forever:
  let us pray to the Lord.

- For television and radio broadcasters,
  for newspaper publishers and editors,
  for journalists and writers,
  for public relations and communications professionals,
  that, through their work,
  justice and truth may be proclaimed "from the housetops":
  let us pray to the Lord.

- [For . . .,
  that . . .:
  let us pray to the Lord.]

- For the sick, the suffering, the recovering, and the dying,
  that the providence of God will be their hope and strength:
  let us pray to the Lord.

- For all of our deceased relatives and friends
  [especially _____],
  that Christ will welcome them into his Father's presence:
  let us pray to the Lord.

- For the prayers we now offer in the silence of our hearts
  [Pause . . .]:
  let us pray to the Lord.

Loving Father, hear our prayers.
Bless us with wisdom
to realize your presence in all good things,
courage to do your will,
and hope to sustain us
as we look forward to the fulfillment
of the promise of the Risen Christ,
in whose name we pray.

(The woman is rewarded for her kindness to the prophet Elisha.)   2 Kings 4:8-11, 14-16

You must consider yourselves dead to sin but alive for God in Christ Jesus.

Romans 6:3-4, 8-11

"He who welcomes you welcomes me."   Matthew 10:37-42

Let us lift up our hearts and voices in prayer
for the needs of all God's people:

- That our Church and parish community
  may be a place of welcome
  to the poor, the troubled, and the lost:
  let us pray to the Lord.

- That those who serve our Church
  as pastors, teachers, and ministers
  may proclaim the victory of Christ crucified:
  let us pray to the Lord.

- That all families, households, and communities
  may find, in Christ,
  neither division nor discord,
  but the source of love, compassion, and reconciliation:
  let us pray to the Lord.

- That those who work to provide human services
  to the poor, the suffering, and the forgotten
  may one day receive "a prophet's reward"
  for their perseverance and commitment:
  let us pray to the Lord.

- [That . . .:
  let us pray to the Lord.]

- That, in our service to the sick,
  the recovering, and the dying,
  we may serve Christ Jesus:
  let us pray to the Lord.

- That God will raise to the new life of Christ
  all who have died in God's peace
  [especially _____]:
  let us pray to the Lord.

- That God will grant the prayers we now make
  in the silence of our hearts
  [Pause . . .]:
  let us pray to the Lord.

O Lord, may the crosses we take up in faith
bring to fulfillment the prayers we have made to you
in the name of our life and hope, Jesus Christ,
who lives and reigns with you for ever and ever.

See, your king shall come to you; a just savior is he.   Zechariah 9:9-10

The Spirit of God dwells in you.   Romans 8:9, 11-13

*"Father, . . . what you have hidden from the learned and the clever you have revealed
to the merest children."*   Matthew 11:25-30

Let us come before the Father in prayer,
in the name of Christ Jesus, our joy and our hope:

- That the Spirit of God may inspire and guide
  every dimension of our life together
  as a Church and parish community:
  let us pray to the Lord.

- That Pope N., Bishop N., Father N.,
  and all who serve the Church
  as bishops, priests, and ministers
  may proclaim God's kindness and love for all humanity:
  let us pray to the Lord.

- That the leaders of nations and governments
  may work together to banish forever
  "the warrior's bow" of war and oppression:
  let us pray to the Lord.

- That we may seek God's simple but profound will
  in all business and public policy decisions:
  let us pray to the Lord.

- [That . . .:
  let us pray to the Lord.]

- That we may welcome to our tables
  the poor, the alienated, the rejected,
  and all who come seeking our help:
  let us pray to the Lord.

- That the souls of the faithful who have died
  [*especially* _____]
  may find rest and peace in the presence of God forever:
  let us pray to the Lord.

- That God will hear the prayers we now make
  in the silence of our hearts
  [Pause . . .]:
  let us pray to the Lord.

As we raise our voices to you in prayer, O God,
raise our spirits to the joy of your presence;
as we lift up our hearts to you in hope,
transform our lives into the glorious life
of your Son, the Risen Christ,
in whose name we offer these prayers.

Just as . . . the rain and snow come down . . . so shall my word be that goes forth.
Isaiah 55:10-11

All creation groans and is in agony even until now. Romans 8:18-23

(The parable of the sower) Matthew 13:1-23

To the God who crowns each year with goodness,
let us lift up our hearts and voices in prayer:

- That our life together as a Church and parish community
  may be rooted in the love and mercy of God:
  let us pray to the Lord.

- That Pope N., Bishop N., Father N.,
  and those who serve us as bishops, priests, and ministers
  may reveal to the Church and the world
  a "knowledge of the mysteries of the reign of God":
  let us pray to the Lord.

- That the nations and peoples of the world
  may work together to protect and share justly
  the many gifts of God's creation:
  let us pray to the Lord.

- That God will bless the work of farmers and food producers
  with a bountiful harvest
  as a blessing for all the human family:
  let us pray to the Lord.

- [That . . .:
  let us pray to the Lord.]

- That those who suffer
  for the sake of what is right and just
  may find hope and inspiration in Christ the Redeemer:
  let us pray to the Lord.

- That those members of our families and parish
who have died in Christ
[especially _____ *]*
may "share in the glorious freedom of the children of God":
let us pray to the Lord.

- That God will hear the prayers we now make
in the silence of our hearts
[Pause . . .]:
let us pray to the Lord.

Gracious God, may these prayers of ours
be seeds of your Spirit in our hearts
that we may work to plant
your mercy, justice, and compassion in our world.
We make these prayers to you
in the name of your Son, our Lord Jesus Christ.

Your might is the source of justice . . . and with much lenience you govern us.
Wisdom 12:13, 16-19

He who searches hearts knows what the Spirit means.   Romans 8:26-27

(The parables of the wheat and weeds, the mustard seed and the yeast)
Matthew 13:24-43

To God, the Father of mercy and the Source of justice,
let us pray:

- That the faith we celebrate at this Eucharistic table
  may make us "wheat" for a world hungering
  for justice and peace:
  let us pray to the Lord.

- That our Church's ministries may teach and proclaim
  neither judgment nor condemnation,
  but the mercy and forgiveness of God:
  let us pray to the Lord.

- That nations, states, and cities
  may find, in God, the Father of all,
  the "source of justice" and the way of peace:
  let us pray to the Lord.

- [That . . .:
  let us pray to the Lord.]

- That the poor, the homeless, the starving,
  and all those in need
  may find a place of honor and compassion among us:
  let us pray to the Lord.

- That the sick, the suffering, and the recovering
  may find hope and healing
  in the God whose love knows no limit:
  let us pray to the Lord.

- That our deceased relatives and friends
  [especially _____]
  may "shine like the sun in their Father's kingdom":
  let us pray to the Lord.

- That the Father "who searches hearts"
  will hear the prayers we now offer
  in the silence of our hearts
  [Pause . . .]:
  let us pray to the Lord.

Father, hear the prayers of your Church.
Let us be
    a wheat of compassion sown amid hatred and injustice;
    a mustard seed of hope for all who come to us in need;
    a yeast of your love to raise up
the grieving, the lost, and the forgotten.
We make these prayers to you
in the name of your Son, our Lord Jesus Christ.

Solomon's request of God: "Give your servant . . . an understanding heart to judge your people." 1 Kings 3:5, 7-12

God makes all things work together for the good of those who love him.
Romans 8:28-30

(The parables of the buried treasure, the pearl, and the dragnet) Matthew 13:44-52

As Paul wrote to the Romans (in today's second reading):
"God makes all things work together
for the good of those who love him."
In confidence, then, let us pray:

- For our Church and parish community,
  that our work and worship together
  may reflect the love and compassion of God:
  let us pray to the Lord.

- For Pope N., Bishop N., Father N.,
  and for all who serve the Church,
  that they may receive hearts of wisdom and understanding
  to lead and serve God's holy people:
  let us pray to the Lord.

- For President N. and Governor N.,
  for judges and court officers,
  for legislators and for all who serve in government,
  that they may carry out their responsibilities
  with wisdom and selflessness:
  let us pray to the Lord.

- For those involved in medical and scientific research,
  that, through their work, humankind may discover anew
  the sacredness of all God's creation:
  let us pray to the Lord.

- For teachers and educators,
  that they may instruct and inspire their students
  to seek the wisdom and understanding of God in all things:
  let us pray to the Lord.

- [For . . .,
  that . . .:
  let us pray to the Lord.]

- For the deceased members of our families and communities
  [*especially* _____],
  that the angels may gather them before the throne of God:
  let us pray to the Lord.

- For the prayers we now make in the silence of our hearts
  [*Pause . . .*]:
  let us pray to the Lord.

God of all goodness, hear the prayers we make to you.
Bless us with the wisdom to recognize your hand at work
in every dimension of our lives;
grant us the faith to understand your will in all things,
so that, in you, our lives may be complete
and our deepest hopes may be fulfilled.
In Jesus' name, we pray.

All you who are thirsty, come to the water! Isaiah 55:1-3

Who will separate us from the love of Christ? Romans 8:35, 37-39

(The miracle of the loaves and fishes) Matthew 14:13-21

To the Lord of kindness and compassion,
to the Lord of justice and mercy,
to the Lord who is near to all,
let us pray:

- For our Church and parish community,
  that we may share joyfully
  with the poor, the hungry, and the forgotten
  all that God has given to us:
  let us pray to the Lord.

- For our bishops, priests, deacons, and ministers,
  that they may teach us that "the Lord is just in all his ways
  and holy in all his works":
  let us pray to the Lord.

- For the leaders of governments and nations,
  that they may work to insure
  the blessings of food, water, and health care
  for every member of the human family:
  let us pray to the Lord.

- For those who grow, produce, and prepare our food,
  that they may see their work
  as a sacred trust from God, the Giver of all good things:
  let us pray to the Lord.

- [For . . .,
  that . . .:
  let us pray to the Lord.]

- For those on the margins of society,
  for cultural and ethnic minorities in our community,
  for those who are physically and mentally challenged,
  that they may find welcome and purpose among us:
  let us pray to the Lord.

- For those who have died in the peace of Christ
  [*especially* _____],
  that they may take their places at the banquet of heaven:
  let us pray to the Lord.

- For the prayers we now make in the silence of our hearts
  [*Pause . . .*]:
  let us pray to the Lord.

In the abundance of your kindness, O Lord, hear our prayers.
May we give you thanks for what you have given us
by giving joyfully to others;
may we embrace your Spirit of love by loving one another,
with selflessness and compassion.
In Jesus' name, we pray.

After the fire [Elijah heard] a tiny whispering sound. 1 Kings 19:9, 11-13

[To the Israelites] were the adoption, the glory, the covenants, the lawgiving,
the worship, and the promises. Romans 9:1-5

"Lord, save me!" Jesus at once stretched out his hand and caught [Peter].
Matthew 14:22-23

We come to this Eucharist with the faith of Peter:
we know that Christ will save us when we call out to him.
With confidence, then, let us call out to the Lord in prayer:

- That we may become a parish community
  bound together by our faith in the certainty
  of God's limitless goodness:
  let us pray to the Lord.

- That Pope N., our bishops, priests, and deacons,
  and all who serve the Church
  may reveal the unseen and unrealized presence of God among us:
  let us pray to the Lord.

- That the nations of the world may listen together
  to hear the Lord's voice of peace and justice:
  let us pray to the Lord.

- That those who make their livelihoods
  from the oceans, seas, and rivers
  may act responsibly to protect and preserve
  God's gift of water:
  let us pray to the Lord.

- [That . . .:
  let us pray to the Lord.]

- That Christ will save and grasp those
  whose lives are battered by storms
  of illness, grief, despair, or addiction:
  let us pray to the Lord.

- That the Risen Christ will bring into his Father's presence
  the souls of those who have died
  [especially _____ *]:*
  let us pray to the Lord.

- That God will hear the prayers we now make
  in the silence of our hearts
  [Pause . . .]:
  let us pray to the Lord.

Lord, our Light and our Hope,
hear the cries of our poor hearts.
Give us the gift of faith
that we may hear you in the quiet of loving compassion,
see you in the kindnesses performed unnoticed around us,
and know your presence in times of anguish and turmoil.
We call out to you,
you who live and reign with the Father,
for ever and ever.

My house shall be called a house of prayer for all peoples. Isaiah 56:1, 6-7

God's gifts and his call are irrevocable. Romans 11:13-15, 29-32

(Jesus cures the daughter of the Canaanite woman.) Matthew 15:21-28

With the confident faith of the Canaanite woman,
let us offer our prayers to the Father in Jesus' name:

- That, in our humble service and welcome to all,
  our Church may be "a house of prayer for all people":
  let us pray to the Lord.

- That those who serve the Church
  as bishops, priests, teachers, and counselors
  may be agents of God's forgiveness
  and ministers of reconciliation:
  let us pray to the Lord.

- That nations and governments
  may initiate and support public policies
  designed to eradicate
  racism, sexism, intolerance, and discrimination
  from all human societies and institutions:
  let us pray to the Lord.

- That our heavenly Father will bless and guide
  mothers and fathers and all who have been called
  to the holy vocation of parenthood:
  let us pray to the Lord.

- [That . . .:
  let us pray to the Lord.]

- That we may imitate the compassion of Christ the Healer
  in our care for the poor,
  the desperate, the addicted, the abused, and the forgotten:
  let us pray to the Lord.

- That God, in love and mercy, will bring into the divine presence
  the souls of all who have died
  [especially _____]:
  let us pray to the Lord.

- That the Father of mercies
  will hear the prayers we now make
  in the silence of our hearts
  [Pause . . .]:
  let us pray to the Lord.

Lord God, may our voices become one
with the voices of all your sons and daughters
throughout the world,
that our common prayer for peace
may be the beginning of a universal commitment
to bring your justice and mercy
to our deeply divided world.
Hear the prayers we make to you
in the name of your Son, our Lord Jesus Christ.

I will place the key of the House of David on [Eliakim's] shoulder. Isaiah 22:15, 19-23

How deep are the riches and the wisdom and the knowledge of God! Romans 11:33-36

"I will entrust to you the keys of the kingdom of heaven." Matthew 16:13-20

God is present to us in this holy assembly.
In joyful hope, then, let us pray:

- For our Church and parish community,
  that we may seek the ways of God in all things:
  let us pray to the Lord.

- For Pope N., Bishop N., Father N.,
  and for all bishops, priests, and ministers,
  that their ministry may be the key that unlocks to all
  the wonder of God's love and mercy:
  let us pray to the Lord.

- For those in government and public service,
  that they may seek the peace and justice of God
  in all human affairs:
  let us pray to the Lord.

- For educators and teachers preparing for a new academic year,
  that they may guide their students in discovering
  "the riches and the wisdom and the knowledge of God":
  let us pray to the Lord.

- [For . . .,
  that . . .:
  let us pray to the Lord.]

- For the sick, the poor, and for all those in need,
  that the care and compassion we extend to them
  may proclaim our faith in Christ, the Son of the living God:
  let us pray to the Lord.

- For all who have died in the peace of Christ
  [especially _____ *],*
  that they may live anew in the light of God's presence:
  let us pray to the Lord.

- For the prayers we now make in the silence of our hearts
  [Pause . . .]:
  let us pray to the Lord.

God our Father,
your great love for us is beyond our imagination,
your wisdom beyond our reasoning.
Give us the gift of faith that *dares* us
    to love one another,
    to forgive one another,
    to be reconciled with one another,
without conditions or limits,
just as you love and forgive us again and again.
Hear these prayers we offer to you in the name of your Son,
our Lord Jesus Christ.

The word of the Lord . . . becomes like fire burning in my heart. Jeremiah 20:7-9

Do not conform yourselves to this age. Romans 12:1-2

"If a man wishes to come after me, he must . . . take up his cross, and begin to follow in my footsteps." Matthew 16:21-27

Let us lift up our hearts and voices to the Lord in prayer:

- For our Church and parish community,
  that we may selflessly take up one another's crosses
  and walk together in the footsteps of Christ:
  let us pray to the Lord.

- For Pope N., Bishop N., Father N.,
  and for all bishops, priests, deacons, and ministers,
  that they may persevere in speaking
  the Word of God burning in their hearts:
  let us pray to the Lord.

- For President N., Governor N.,
  and all legislators, judges, and government officials,
  that they may conduct the affairs of state
  by God's standards of justice and equality:
  let us pray to the Lord.

- [For . . .,
  that . . .:
  let us pray to the Lord.]

- For those who serve and advocate
  for the poor, the oppressed, and all in need,
  that we may hear, in their cry for justice,
  the Word of God:
  let us pray to the Lord.

- For the sick, the suffering, the recovering, and the dying,
  that they may find hope and healing
  in our compassionate care and support:
  let us pray to the Lord.

- For the faithful who have died
  [*especially* _____],
  that they may be welcomed by the angels
  into the kingdom of God:
  let us pray to the Lord.

- For the prayers we now make in the silence of our hearts
  [*Pause . . .*]:
  let us pray to the Lord.

O Lord, hear our prayers for the human family.
Give us eyes to see your face
    in the midst of suffering and anguish;
give us ears to hear your voice
    in the midst of ridicule and confusion;
give us hearts that sense your presence
    in times of turmoil and despair.
In Jesus' name, we pray.

When you hear me say anything, you shall warn them for me.   Ezekiel 33:7-9

Love never does any wrong to the neighbor, hence love is the fulfillment of the law.
                                                                      Romans 13:8-10

"Where two or three are gathered in my name, there am I in their midst."
                                                                      Matthew 18:15-20

Whenever "two or three are gathered in [his] name,"
Jesus has assured us of his presence.
Confident of his presence among us now, let us pray:

- That our Church and parish community
  may seek the love of God in all things:
  let us pray to the Lord.

- That our bishops, priests, deacons, and ministers
  may teach the gospel of forgiveness
  with conviction and compassion:
  let us pray to the Lord.

- That the legislatures and courts of the world's governments
  may seek equality, justice, and peace for all peoples:
  let us pray to the Lord.

- [That . . .:
  let us pray to the Lord.]

- That the Jesus of love and compassion
  may be present in the midst of families and households,
  especially those experiencing times of difficulty and pain:
  let us pray to the Lord.

- That the sick and suffering,
  the poor and broken,
  the grieving and despondent,
  may find, among us, reconciling hope and healing:
  let us pray to the Lord.

- That our deceased relatives and friends
  [especially _____]
  may be raised by God to the new life of the Risen Christ:
  let us pray to the Lord.

- That God will hear the prayers we now make
  in the silence of our hearts
  [Pause . . .]:
  let us pray to the Lord.

In your name, O Lord, we gather in prayer.
Your presence in our midst
makes our gathering here a *holy* assembly.
May we take your holy presence from this place
into our homes, schools, and workplaces.
We offer these prayers in the name of Christ Jesus,
who lives and reigns with you as the one God,
for ever and ever.

The vengeful will suffer the Lord's vengeance, for he remembers their sins in detail.
Sirach 27:30–28:7

Both in life and in death we are the Lord's.
Romans 14:7-9

(The parable of the unforgiving servant)
Matthew 18:21-35

In the name of Christ—
    the Lord of the living and the dead,
    the Savior of the rich and the poor,
    the Hope of saints and sinners—
let us raise our hearts and voices in prayer to God:

- For our Church and parish community,
  that we may share willingly and justly
  all that God has given us
  with the poor and those in need:
  let us pray to the Lord.

- For Pope N., Bishop N., Father N.,
  and all who serve our Church,
  that they may joyfully preach
  the gospel of the Resurrection:
  let us pray to the Lord.

- For the leaders of nations, states, and cities,
  that they may work to establish
  the justice and mercy of God
  through all the earth:
  let us pray to the Lord.

- For families and communities
  suffering from division, alienation, and estrangement,
  that they may put aside anger and hate
  and seek together forgiveness and reconciliation:
  let us pray to the Lord.

- [For . . .,
  that . . .:
  let us pray to the Lord.]

- For the sick, the suffering, and the dying,
  that the kindness and compassion of God may shine upon them:
  let us pray to the Lord.

- For the faithful who have died
  [especially _____ *],*
  that Christ may claim their souls
  for the kingdom of his Father:
  let us pray to the Lord.

- For the prayers we now make in the silence of our hearts
  [Pause . . .]:
  let us pray to the Lord.

Lord God, may these prayers be our first step
in removing anger and hatred from our world
and bringing your limitless love and unconditional forgiveness
into our homes, our schools, our parish, and our community.
We make these prayers to you
in the name of your Son, Jesus Christ,
who lives and reigns with you for ever and ever.

As high as the heavens are above the earth, so high are my ways above your ways.
Isaiah 55:6-9

Christ will be exalted through me, whether I live or die. For, to me, "life" means Christ.
Philippians 1:20-24, 27

"The last shall be first and the first shall be last."   Matthew 20:1-16

To God, the Father of mercy and forgiveness, let us pray:

- That, as a Church and parish community,
  we may joyfully imitate the limitless generosity of God
  in every dimension of our life together:
  let us pray to the Lord.

- That the Risen Christ may be "exalted" in the ministries
  of the bishops, priests, deacons, and teachers of our Church:
  let us pray to the Lord.

- That the public policies of the world's nations and cities
  may seek to uphold the dignity of every man, woman, and child
  as sons and daughters of God:
  let us pray to the Lord.

- [That . . .:
  let us pray to the Lord.]

- That we may work to repair broken relationships
  and tear down walls of misunderstanding and mistrust
  that separate us from others:
  let us pray to the Lord.

- That we may rejoice and welcome into the "vineyard"
  those who have recovered and restored their lives
  in the grace and peace of God:
  let us pray to the Lord.

- That Christ Jesus will raise up
  to the new life of his resurrection
  the souls of the faithful who have died
  [*especially* _____]:
  let us pray to the Lord.

- That the God of love and mercy will hear the prayers
  we now make in the silence of our hearts
  [Pause . . .]:
  let us pray to the Lord.

God our Father,
open our minds that we might comprehend
the depth of your love for all men, women, and children;
open our eyes that we might realize
your vision of peace and justice for the world you made;
open our hearts that we might forgive those who hurt us
and seek the forgiveness of those we hurt.
Hear our prayers that your graciousness and holiness
may be reflected in each one of us.
In Jesus' name, we pray.

Is it my way that is unfair, or rather, are not your ways unfair? Ezekiel 18:25-28

Your attitude must be Christ's. Philippians 2:1-11

"Tax collectors and prostitutes are entering the kingdom of God before you."
Matthew 21:28-32

It is difficult for us to comprehend
the limitless depth of God's great love and compassion.
But while filling us with wonder,
it also enlivens us with hope.
With joyful confidence, then, let us pray:

- For our Church and parish,
  that we may become a community
  of solace, encouragement, and compassion:
  let us pray to the Lord.

- For pastors and preachers,
  for teachers and catechists,
  that they may lead their hearers in the ways of God:
  let us pray to the Lord.

- For the nations and peoples of the world,
  that they may seek to be the humble servants of one another,
  "looking to others' interests" rather than their own:
  let us pray to the Lord.

- For children and young people,
  that they may always possess the joy and wonder
  of God's great love and care for them:
  let us pray to the Lord.

- [For . . .,
  that . . .:
  let us pray to the Lord.]

- For those who are enslaved by any form of addiction,
  for those who are embittered or lost in despair,
  for those who are struggling to rebuild their lives,
  that our support and compassion for them
  may be a light of hope and renewal:
  let us pray to the Lord.

- For our deceased relatives and friends
  [especially _____ *],*
  that Christ will welcome them into the kingdom of his Father:
  let us pray to the Lord.

- For the prayers we now offer in the silence of our hearts
  [Pause . . .]:
  let us pray to the Lord.

So great is your love for us, O Lord,
that you humbled yourself to become one of us.
May we embrace Christ's attitude of humility and compassion:
like him, may we welcome the lost and rejected to our table;
like him, may we seek the needs of others before our own;
like him, may we rejoice in forgiveness and reconciliation
    before demanding judgment and condemnation.
In Jesus' name, we pray.

(Isaiah's song of his friend's vineyard) Isaiah 5:1-7

Live according to what you have learned and accepted. Philippians 4:6-9

(The parable of the evil tenants and the vineyard)
"The stone . . . has become the keystone of the structure." Matthew 21:33-43

In prayer and gratitude,
let us present our needs to God in Jesus' name:

- That Christ may be the "keystone" of our life together
  as a Church and parish community:
  let us pray to the Lord.

- That the teaching and preaching ministry
  of Pope N. and our bishops, priests, and ministers
  may yield a harvest of compassion and reconciliation:
  let us pray to the Lord.

- That the nations and cities of the world
  may make of the earth
  a vineyard of peace, justice, and equality:
  let us pray to the Lord.

- [That . . .:
  let us pray to the Lord.]

- That those who grieve and mourn,
  whose lives are shattered
  and whose spirits and broken
  may find consolation, purpose, and hope among us:
  let us pray to the Lord.

- That the sick, the suffering, and the dying
  may experience anew the life of Christ:
  let us pray to the Lord.

- That those who have died in the peace of Christ
  [*especially* _____]
  may take their places in the kingdom of God:
  let us pray to the Lord.

- That God will hear the prayers we now make
  in the silence of our hearts
  [Pause . . .]:
  let us pray to the Lord.

Hear our prayers, O Lord,
for our families, our Church, our nation, and our world.
May our compassion for the poor and the needy,
our service to our brothers and sisters,
and our respect for all your people
make us worthy tenants of your kingdom to come.
We offer our prayers to you in the name of your Son,
our Lord and Savior, Jesus Christ.

---

*On this mountain the Lord of hosts will provide for all peoples a feast of rich foods
and choice wines.*   Isaiah 25:6-10

In him who is the source of my strength I have strength for everything.
                                                    Philippians 4:12-14, 19-20

(The parable of the wedding banquet for the king's son)   Matthew 22:1-14

Before we celebrate the Eucharist of Christ the Bridegroom,
let us raise our hearts and voices in prayer
for everyone God invites to the Eucharistic table:

- That Isaiah's vision of a world united in God
  may begin in our own homes and parish community:
  let us pray to the Lord.

- That our Church's pastors, ministers, and teachers
  may lead us and all peoples to God's holy mountain:
  let us pray to the Lord.

- That legislatures, courts, and agencies of government
  may work to provide all peoples
  with a just share of the world's harvest:
  let us pray to the Lord.

- [That . . .:
  let us pray to the Lord.]

- That, with love and compassion,
  we may welcome the poor and needy
  to our altars and banquet tables:
  let us pray to the Lord.

- That the sick, the lost, and the addicted
  may realize the strength they possess
  in the One who is the source of all strength:
  let us pray to the Lord.

- That the Father will welcome to the wedding feast of the Son
  the souls of the faithful who have died
  [especially _____]:
  let us pray to the Lord.

- That God will hear the prayers we now make
  in the silence of our hearts
  [Pause . . .]:
  let us pray to the Lord.

Father, we thank you for welcoming us to your banquet.
May our attitudes reflect the joy and hope of your invitation;
may the good that we do for others
weave a proper garment for us to wear
at the wedding feast of your Son, our Lord Jesus Christ,
in whose name we offer these prayers.

It is I who arm you, though you know me not. Isaiah 45:1, 4-6

Our preaching of the gospel proved not a mere matter of words but one of power.
1 Thessalonians 1:1-5

"Give to Caesar what is Caesar's, but give to God what is God's." Matthew 22:15-21

With thanksgiving for God's goodness
and with hope in God's continued providence,
let us offer our prayers:

- For our Church and parish community,
  that, in our life together,
  we may seek God's will in all things:
  let us pray to the Lord.

- For Pope N., Bishop N., Father N.,
  and for all who serve our Church,
  that their preaching of the gospel
  may be "not a mere matter of words"
  but a proclamation of joyful conviction:
  let us pray to the Lord.

- For President N., Governor N.,
  and for all who govern and lead,
  that they may uphold the sacred dignity
  of every man, woman, and child:
  let us pray to the Lord.

- For theologians and ethicists,
  that they may challenge society
  to recognize the hand of God in all human affairs:
  let us pray to the Lord.

- [For . . .,
  that . . .:
  let us pray to the Lord.]

- For those on the fringes of society,
  for the rejected, the scorned, and the lost,
  that we may accept our responsibility to them
  as an expression of our faith in the Jesus of the Gospels:
  let us pray to the Lord.

- For all who have died in the peace of Christ
  [especially _____],
  that they will be raised up
  to the new life of God's Risen Son:
  let us pray to the Lord.

- For the prayers we now make in the silence of our hearts
  [Pause . . .]:
  let us pray to the Lord.

May the prayers we offer to you, O God,
be more than a matter of words:
may they be a conviction of spirit
that celebrates and reveals your presence
in every place and time.
Father, hear these prayers which we make to you
in the name of your Son,
our Lord and Savior, Jesus Christ.

*"If you ever wrong [any widow or orphan] and they ever cry out to me,
I will surely hear their cry."* Exodus 22:20-26

The word of the Lord has echoed forth from you resoundingly. 1 Thessalonians 1:5-10

"On these two commandments the whole law is based, and the prophets as well." Matthew 22:34-40

To God, the Source of everything that is good, let us pray:

- That the gospel principles of love and compassion for all
  may be the heart of our life together
  as a Church and parish community:
  let us pray to the Lord.

- That God's word of compassion and reconciliation
  may echo forth resoundingly
  in the teaching and ministry
  of Pope N., and our bishops, priests, and deacons:
  let us pray to the Lord.

- That nations and governments may find ways
  to break down the barriers and tear down the walls
  that divide families and communities:
  let us pray to the Lord.

- [That . . .:
  let us pray to the Lord.]

- That families experiencing hardship, turmoil, or loss
  may be strengthened by the loving support of one another
  and of friends and neighbors:
  let us pray to the Lord.

- That our compassion and kindness
  to the sick, the poor, and those in need
  may make us worthy to be remembered
  in *their* prayers to God:
  let us pray to the Lord.

- That the Risen Christ may bring into the presence of his Father
  the souls of our deceased relatives and friends
  [especially _____ *]:*
  let us pray to the Lord.

- That God will hear the prayers we now make
  in the silence of our hearts
  [Pause . . .]:
  let us pray to the Lord.

Gracious God, Author of all love,
may your rule of compassion
and commandment of love
govern every moment of life you give us
until the coming of your reign,
where Jesus is Lord for ever and ever.

Have we not all the one Father? Why then do we break faith with each other?
Malachi 1:14–2:2, 8-10

We wanted to share with you not only God's tidings but our very lives.
1 Thessalonians 2:7-9, 13

"The greatest among you will be the one who serves the rest." Matthew 23:1-12

The Lord is our hope and our peace.
In confidence, then, let us pray:

- That we may keep faith with one another
  in our life together as a parish community:
  let us pray to the Lord.

- That pastors, ministers, and religious educators
  may proclaim, through their humility and selflessness,
  the good tidings of God's great mercy and love:
  let us pray to the Lord.

- That nations and societies may honor
  the dignity that all men, women, and children possess
  as children of the same God and Father:
  let us pray to the Lord.

- That parents and guardians
  may love and care for their children
  as the Father in heaven loves and cares for all humanity as sons
    and daughters of God:
  let us pray to the Lord.

- [That . . .:
  let us pray to the Lord.]

- That the sick, the recovering, and the dying
  may be reassured of the love of God
  in the love and care we joyfully extend to them:
  let us pray to the Lord.

- That the deceased members of our families and parish
  [especially _____]
  may live anew in the light and peace of the Risen Christ:
  let us pray to the Lord.

- That God will hear the prayers we now make
  in the silence of our hearts
  [Pause . . .]:
  let us pray to the Lord.

With one heart and one voice,
we come before you, O God.
May we be worthy to be called your sons and daughters
by serving our brothers and sisters
with compassion and care,
in imitation of Jesus Christ, your Son,
in whose name we offer these prayers.

Resplendent and unfading is Wisdom, and she is readily perceived by those who love her, and found by those who seek her. Wisdom 6:12-16

God will bring forth with him from the dead those who have fallen asleep believing in him. 1 Thessalonians 4:13-17

(The parable of the ten bridesmaids) Matthew 25:1-13

To the Lord, who is our hope and our joy, let us pray:

- For our parish community,
  that our prayers and ministries may be a sign of hope
  in the reign of God to come:
  let us pray to the Lord.

- For Pope N., Bishop N., Father N.,
  and for all who serve the Church,
  that they may proclaim God's Word of hope and consolation
  to our broken world:
  let us pray to the Lord.

- For President N., Governor N.,
  for legislators and judges,
  and for all who serve in government,
  that the wisdom of God may guide them
  in their service to their people:
  let us pray to the Lord.

- For teachers and students,
  for scholars and researchers,
  for scientists and explorers,
  that their work may lead us all to a deeper understanding
  of the wonders and wisdom of God:
  let us pray to the Lord.

- For hospital chaplains and hospice workers,
  and for all who care for the sick and dying,
  that they may be a source of hope and comfort
  to those in their care:
  let us pray to the Lord.

- [For . . .,
  that . . .:
  let us pray to the Lord.]

- For all who have died in the peace of Christ
  [especially _____ *],*
  that they will be welcomed into the presence of God forever:
  let us pray to the Lord.

- For the prayers we now offer in the silence of our hearts
  [Pause . . .]:
  let us pray to the Lord.

O Lord, you are our hope, who will never leave us disappointed;
you are our joy, who turns our mourning into dancing;
you are our Father, whose love knows neither limit nor condition.
With humility and hope,
with the conviction of faith,
with the joy you inspire,
we offer these prayers for all your holy people
in the name of your Son, our Lord Jesus Christ.

The woman who fears the Lord is to be praised. Proverbs 31:10-13, 19-20, 30-31

All of you are children of light and of the day. 1 Thessalonians 5:1-6

(The parable of the talents) Matthew 25:14-30

With gratitude for the blessings we have received
and with hope in the promise to come,
let us raise our hearts in prayer to the Lord:

- For our Church and parish community,
  that our work and worship may reflect
  our call to be ''children of light'':
  let us pray to the Lord.

- For the nations and peoples of the world,
  that they may be dedicated to building peace
  and to the faithful stewardship of the earth's harvest:
  let us pray to the Lord.

- For married couples,
  that they may always live their life together
  as a sacrament of Christ's loving presence:
  let us pray to the Lord.

- For businesses and financial institutions,
  that they may conduct their affairs
  with integrity and justice:
  let us pray to the Lord.

- [For . . .,
  that . . .:
  let us pray to the Lord.]

- For the sick, the suffering, the recovering, and the dying,
  that God's love may be present to them
  in the care and support we extend to them:
  let us pray to the Lord.

- For the members of our families and parish who have died
  [especially _____ *],*
  that the peace and light of the Risen Christ may be theirs:
  let us pray to the Lord.

- For the prayers we now offer in the silence of our hearts
  [Pause . . .]:
  let us pray to the Lord.

Lord God, you have given us the blessing of life itself—
    health, intellect, talents, and abilities;
you have blessed us with this good earth—
    a harvest of food, resources to warm us and protect us;
you have enlivened us with the gift of faith—
    enabling us to love, giving us reason to hope.
May we be worthy stewards of these gifts
that we may use them to the glory of your name.
In Jesus' name, we pray.

I myself will look after and tend my sheep.   Ezekiel 34:11-12, 15-17

Christ has been raised from the dead, the first fruits of those who have fallen asleep.
                                                        1 Corinthians 15:20-26, 28

"The king will answer them: '. . . as often as you did it for one of my least brothers, you did it for me.' "   Matthew 25:31-46

In joyful hope,
let us come before God
in the name of our King, Jesus Christ.

- That our Church and parish community may be a place
  where the poor are honored,
  the rejected are welcomed,
  and the sick and recovering are cared for:
  let us pray to the Lord.

- That Pope N., Bishop N., Father N.,
  and the bishops, priests, and ministers of our Church
  may imitate the servanthood of Christ Jesus:
  let us pray to the Lord.

- That President N., Governor N.,
  and all legislators, judges, and government officials
  may serve our nation and state with wisdom and compassion:
  let us pray to the Lord.

- [That . . .:
  let us pray to the Lord.]

- That those who provide for the poor,
  who console the troubled and the grieving,
  who care for the sick and the dying,
  may inherit the "kingdom" prepared for them:
  let us pray to the Lord.

- That we may see,
  in the faces of the homeless, the hungry, the sick,
  the abused, and the addicted,
  the face of Christ Jesus:
  let us pray to the Lord.

- That our deceased relatives and friends
  [especially _____]
  may share in the promise of Christ's resurrection:
  let us pray to the Lord.

- That our Father in heaven will hear the prayers
  we now offer in the silence of our hearts
  [Pause . . .]:
  let us pray to the Lord.

We praise you, O God,
you who are Lord of all creation
and Father of all nations.
Hear the prayers we offer in joyful hope
as we await the coming of our Messiah and King, Jesus Christ,
who lives and reigns with you and the Holy Spirit
as the one God,
for ever and ever.

YEAR B

No ear has ever heard, no eye ever seen, any God but you.   Isaiah 63:16-17, 19; 64:2-7

I continually thank my God for you.   1 Corinthians 1:3-9

"You do not know when the master of the house is coming."   Mark 13:33-37

"No ear has ever heard, no eye has ever seen"
greater wonders than what God has done for us.
With confidence, then,
let us offer our prayers to God, our Father and Redeemer:

- That our prayer and work together
  as a Church and parish community
  may reflect our joyful expectation of Christ's coming:
  let us pray to the Lord.

- That the ministries of the Church
  and the policies of governments and nations
  may transform discord into cooperation,
  hatred into peace,
  and distrust into respect and understanding:
  let us pray to the Lord.

- That this Advent season may be a time
  not for mindless consumerism
  but for the renewal and re-creation of human hearts:
  let us pray to the Lord.

- [That . . .:
  let us pray to the Lord.]

- That families in crisis
  and families who are divided and separated from one another
  may find healing and reconciliation in this Advent journey:
  let us pray to the Lord.

- That those who are mired in despair,
  who are abandoned or turned away,
  may see the face of God in our compassionate outreach to them:
  let us pray to the Lord.

- That Christ will bring into his Father's presence
  the souls of our deceased relatives and friends
  [especially _____]:
  let us pray to the Lord.

- That God will grant, in kindness and mercy,
  the prayers we now make in the silence of our hearts
  [Pause . . .]:
  let us pray to the Lord.

You, O Lord, are the Potter
and we are the clay, the work of your hands.
Shape us in your ways of justice and mercy,
form us in your peace,
and craft us in your love.
We ask these things in the name of your Son, our Savior, Jesus Christ.

Comfort, give comfort to my people.   Isaiah 40:1-5, 9-11

What we await are new heavens and a new earth.   2 Peter 3:8-14

John the Baptizer appeared in the desert proclaiming a baptism of repentance.

Mark 1:1-8

In joyful hope in the coming of God's reign,
let us pray:

- For our Church and our parish community,
  that in our prayer and work together
  we may create a highway for our God:
  let us pray to the Lord.

- For our bishops, priests, deacons,
  and for all who serve the Church,
  that they may proclaim
  the comforting and healing mercy of God:
  let us pray to the Lord.

- For those who lead and govern,
  that they may be instruments
  of God's peace and justice for all peoples:
  let us pray to the Lord.

- For all Churches and faith communities,
  that they may be heralds of the good news
  of God's presence among us:
  let us pray to the Lord.

- [For . . .,
  that . . .:
  let us pray to the Lord.]

- For the poor, the homeless, and the forgotten,
  that we may recognize, in them, the person of Jesus:
  let us pray to the Lord.

- For all our deceased relatives and friends
  [especially _____ *],*
  that Christ the Shepherd may gather them
  into his care forever:
  let us pray to the Lord.

- For the prayers we now make in the silence of our hearts
  [Pause . . .]:
  let us pray to the Lord.

Lord God, hear the prayers of your people
who anxiously await your coming.
Help us to straighten the crooked roads of our lives
so that we might create a highway
for you to enter our homes and hearts
with the peace of Christ Jesus, your Son,
in whose name we offer these prayers.

The Lord God [will] make justice and praise spring up before all the nations.

Isaiah 61:1-2, 10-11

Rejoice always, never cease praying, render constant thanks. 1 Thessalonians 5:16-24

John [was] sent by God, . . . as a witness to testify to the light. John 1:6-8, 19-28

Let us now offer our prayers in joyful hope to the Lord
who comes to heal us and save us:

- For our Church and parish community,
  that joy and thanksgiving may be the center
  of the faith we live and celebrate together:
  let us pray to the Lord.

- For Pope N., Bishop N., Father N.,
  and for all bishops, priests, and deacons,
  that they may be faithful witnesses to the light of Christ:
  let us pray to the Lord.

- For the peoples and countries of the world,
  that justice, liberty, and peace
  may "spring up" before all nations:
  let us pray to the Lord.

- For families and households,
  that the joy and peace of this holy season
  may illuminate their homes
  in every season of the year:
  let us pray to the Lord.

- [For . . .,
  that . . .:
  let us pray to the Lord.]

- For those who fear, who suffer, and who mourn,
  that, in our compassion and help,
  they may experience the healing presence of God:
  let us pray to the Lord.

- For all the faithful who have died
  [*especially* _____],
  that they may be reborn in the light of the Risen Savior:
  let us pray to the Lord.

- For the prayers we now make in the silence of our hearts
  [*Pause . . .*]:
  let us pray to the Lord.

Gracious God, hear our prayers.
May your Spirit come upon us
to transform our lives and our world
    from barrenness to harvest,
    from sickness to wholeness,
    from division to completeness,
    from death to life.
We ask this in the name of Jesus, our Savior and Redeemer.

(The Lord will establish David's house and kingdom forever.)
2 Samuel 7:1-5, 8-11, 14, 16

May glory be given [to God] through Jesus Christ unto endless ages.   Romans 16:25-27

"You shall conceive and bear a son and give him the name Jesus. . . .
His reign will be without end."
Luke 1:26-38

In joyful anticipation of the Lord's coming at Christmas,
let us join our hearts and voices in prayer:

- For our Church and parish community,
  that we may joyfully respond to the will of God
  with the faith and trust of Mary:
  let us pray to the Lord.

- For all pastors and ministers of our Church,
  that they may reveal,
  in their humble and dedicated service,
  the mystery of God's great love for all humanity:
  let us pray to the Lord.

- For the nations and peoples of the world,
  that the reign of God's peace may be established forever:
  let us pray to the Lord.

- For all parents and guardians of children,
  that they may see in Mary
  a model of loving patience and selfless devotion:
  let us pray to the Lord.

- For those who do not celebrate Christ's birth,
  that they, too, may know
  the joy and peace of the Messiah's coming:
  let us pray to the Lord.

- [For . . .,
  that . . .:
  let us pray to the Lord.]

- For our deceased relatives and friends
  [*especially* _____],
  that they may dwell forever in the house of God:
  let us pray to the Lord.

- For the prayers we now make in the silence of our hearts
  [*Pause . . .*]:
  let us pray to the Lord.

Come, Lord God,
shatter the darkness of our world
with the light of your love.
May these prayers we offer
and our work to bring them to fulfillment
bring the light and peace of the Messiah
into our own time and place.
We ask this in the name of our hope, Jesus, the Christ.

The Sundays and Feasts of
THE CHRISTMAS SEASON

See Year A.

ASH WEDNESDAY

See Year A.

137

(God's covenant with Noah) Genesis 9:8-15

Christ died for sins . . . so that he might lead you to God. 1 Peter 3:18-22

Jesus . . . stayed in the wasteland forty days, put to the test there by Satan.
Mark 1:12-15

To the Lord of compassion and mercy,
let us offer our prayers:

- That these forty days of Lent may be
  a desert experience for each of us
  to rediscover the ways of God:
  let us pray to the Lord.

- That all who serve the Church
  as pastors, ministers, and teachers
  may effectively proclaim the reign of God:
  let us pray to the Lord.

- That those who govern nations and human destinies
  may be committed to the justice and mercy of God,
  working unceasingly for the alleviation
  of hunger and misery in our world:
  let us pray to the Lord.

- That, in making moral and ethical choices,
  we may not bow before money, power, and prestige,
  but place our hope in the saving Word of God:
  let us pray to the Lord.

- [That . . .:
  let us pray to the Lord.]

- That our compassionate Father in heaven will watch over those
  who have been displaced from their homes
  by disaster, persecution, or financial hardship:
  let us pray to the Lord.

- That all who have died
  [especially _____]
  and those who will return to God during this Lenten season
  may experience the eternal life of the victorious Christ:
  let us pray to the Lord.

- That God will hear the prayers we now offer
  in the silence of our hearts
  [Pause . . .]:
  let us pray to the Lord.

Hear the prayers we offer to you, O Lord.
During these holy days of Lent,
may we dedicate ourselves to the work
of making these prayers a reality.
We ask these things of you
in the name of Jesus, our Redeemer.

(Abraham does not withhold from the Lord his beloved son.)

Genesis 22:1-2, 9, 10-13, 15-18

If God is for us, who can be against us? Romans 8:31-34

Jesus . . . was transfigured before their eyes and his clothes became dazzling.

Mark 9:2-10

Let us join our hearts and voices in prayer
that God may transform us in love and peace:

- For our Church and parish community,
  that, in our prayer and work together,
  ''the earth shall find blessing'' in us:
  let us pray to the Lord.

- For all nations and peoples,
  that they may work together to re-create our world
  in the justice and peace of God:
  let us pray to the Lord.

- For parents and guardians,
  that their children may discover
  in their love and care for them
  the loving providence of God:
  let us pray to the Lord.

- For those who are preparing for baptism
  and reception into the Church,
  that their hearts may be opened to the Word of God's own Son:
  let us pray to the Lord.

- [For . . .,
  that . . .:
  let us pray to the Lord.]

- For those experiencing loss or crisis in their lives,
  that, with our compassionate support and kindness,
  they may transform their heartache into joy,
  their despair into hope:
  let us pray to the Lord.

- For all the faithful who have died
  [especially _____],
  that they may walk forever in the presence of God:
  let us pray to the Lord.

- For the prayers we now make in the silence of our hearts
  [Pause . . .]:
  let us pray to the Lord.

Father, hear the prayers we make before you.
May your Spirit of compassion and peace
transfigure us and our world
into the image of Jesus, the Risen Christ,
in whose name we offer these prayers.

(God delivers his commandments to Moses and the Israelites.) Exodus 20:1-17

We preach Christ crucified, a stumbling block to Jews and an absurdity to Gentiles.
1 Corinthians 1:22-25

"Destroy this temple . . . and in three days I will raise it up." John 2:13-25

To the God of goodness and compassion,
let us pray for our Church, for our world, and for one another:

- That our parish may be the "Father's house"—
  a dwelling place of God's compassion and love:
  let us pray to the Lord.

- That the Churches and faith communities of the Christian world
  may look beyond their different expressions of belief
  and celebrate together the wisdom and love of God:
  let us pray to the Lord.

- That the work of scientists and medical researchers
  may enhance our respect for nature
  and our gratitude to God for the wonders of creation:
  let us pray to the Lord.

- That couples and families
  experiencing difficult times in their life together
  may realize anew the presence of Christ in their midst:
  let us pray to the Lord.

- [That . . .:
  let us pray to the Lord.]

- That we may imitate the crucified Christ
  in our selfless outreach
  to the poor, the forgotten, and the abandoned:
  let us pray to the Lord.

- That all who have died
  [especially _____]
  and those who will return to God during this Lenten season
  may share in the eternal victory of the Risen Christ:
  let us pray to the Lord.

- That God will hear the prayers we now offer
  in the silence of our hearts
  [Pause . . .]:
  let us pray to the Lord.

We come before you, O God,
with open and humble hearts.
Give us the vision to seek you in all things,
that our lives may be made complete in your joy
and made whole in your compassionate love.
Hear these prayers we ask of you
in the name of Jesus, our Redeemer.

(Cyrus releases God's people to return to Jerusalem to rebuild the Lord's house.)
2 Chronicles 36:14-17, 19-23

We are truly [God's] handiwork, created in Christ Jesus. Ephesians 2:4-10

"Just as Moses lifted up the serpent in the desert, so must the Son of Man be lifted up, so that all who believe may have eternal life in him." John 3:14-21

To our God, who is rich in mercy,
whose love for us is immeasurable,
let us offer our prayers:

- For our Church and parish community,
  that God's love may show forth in our life together:
  let us pray to the Lord.

- For Pope N., Bishop N., Father N.,
  and all who serve the Church as pastors and ministers,
  that they may speak the life-giving, loving voice of God:
  let us pray to the Lord.

- For those who develop and govern matters of public policy,
  that the sacred dignity that every person possesses
  by virtue of being God's "handiwork"
  may be protected and honored:
  let us pray to the Lord.

- For those who fight for justice,
  that their uncompromising witness
  may inspire us to seek God's mercy and justice
  in all things, for all people:
  let us pray to the Lord.

- For those separated from their families and homes
  by war, famine, or catastrophe,
  that, under God's providence,
  they may be reunited quickly and safely:
  let us pray to the Lord.

- [For . . .,
  that . . .:
  let us pray to the Lord.]

- For all who have died
  [especially _____ *],*
  that they may awake and arise in the light of Christ:
  let us pray to the Lord.

- For the prayers we now offer in the silence of our hearts
  [Pause . . .]:
  let us pray to the Lord.

May the prayers we lift before you
be the stones of our temple of praise to you, O Lord;
may our acts of compassion and selflessness
build us into the body of Christ, your beloved Son,
in whose name we offer these prayers.

The days are coming, says the Lord, when I will make a new covenant with the house of Israel.   Jeremiah 31:31-34

(Christ learned obedience from what he suffered.)   Hebrews 5:7-9

"The grain of wheat [that] falls to the earth and dies . . . produces much fruit."
                                                       John 12:20-33

With the same hope and confidence we have
that winter will be transformed into spring
and that the grain of wheat will yield its harvest,
let us offer our prayers to God in Jesus' name:

- That, in our common life together,
  our Church and parish community
  may proclaim the life and love of God:
  let us pray to the Lord.

- That those who serve the Church
  as bishops, priests, deacons, and ministers
  may imitate the humble obedience of Christ Jesus:
  let us pray to the Lord.

- That the wisdom and justice of God
  may be the foundation of all laws and public policies
  enacted by the world's nations, states, and governments:
  let us pray to the Lord.

- That those who are entombed
  by illness, substance abuse, violence, or fear
  may be raised up to a new life of hope and fulfillment:
  let us pray to the Lord.

- [That . . .:
  let us pray to the Lord.]

- That all who grieve and mourn,
  who are suffering the pain of broken relationships,
  may experience God's presence in our loving care and support:
  let us pray to the Lord.

146

- That those who have gone before us
  marked with the sign of faith
  [*especially* _____]
  may find light, happiness, and peace
  in the presence of the Risen Christ:
  let us pray to the Lord.

- That God will hear the prayers we now offer
  in the silence of our hearts
  [*Pause . . .*]:
  let us pray to the Lord.

God of life, Source of love,
accept the offering of our prayers.
Bless us always with the hope of the grain of wheat,
that we may seek to die to ourselves for the sake of others
so that we may one day rise to the new life
of the eternal springtime of your Son,
our Lord and Risen Savior, Jesus Christ,
who lives and reigns with you for ever and ever.

PALM SUNDAY

See Year A.

THE EASTER TRIDUUM

See Year A.

EASTER SUNDAY

See Year A.

None of them ever claimed anything as his own; rather everything was held in common.
Acts 4:32-35

Everyone who believes that Jesus is the Christ has been begotten by God. 1 John 5:1-6

[Jesus said] to Thomas: "Do not persist in your unbelief, but believe!" John 20:19-31

In peace—the peace of the Risen Jesus—let us pray:

- For our Church and our parish,
  that our Easter celebration may make us
  a community united in faith,
  prayer, and the breaking of bread:
  let us pray to the Lord.

- For Pope N., Bishop N., Father N.,
  and for all who lead and serve the Church,
  that they may be ministers of forgiveness
  and prophets of peace:
  let us pray to the Lord.

- For all Christian Churches and communities,
  that they may accomplish great things
  through the faith they share in Jesus, the Risen One:
  let us pray to the Lord.

- For all nations and peoples,
  that the gift of Christ's peace may be theirs:
  let us pray to the Lord.

- [For . . .,
  that . . .:
  let us pray to the Lord.]

- For the sick, the recovering, and the struggling,
  that we may bring healing to their lives
  through our compassion and care:
  let us pray to the Lord.

- For the faithful who have died
  [especially _____],
  that they may be reborn in the life of the Risen Christ:
  let us pray to the Lord.

- For the prayers we now make in the silence of our hearts
  [Pause . . .]:
  let us pray to the Lord.

Grant us, O Lord, your peace:
the peace that enables us to constantly discover your joy;
the peace that impels us to seek your justice in all things;
the peace that allows us to suffer for what is right and good;
the peace that invites us to call
    every man, woman, and child "friend."
Hear the prayers we offer for peace—
the peace of Jesus Christ, our Lord and Risen Savior,
who lives and reigns with you for ever and ever.

Peter said to the people: . . . "God raised [Jesus] from the dead, and we are his witnesses."   Acts 3:13-15, 17-19

We have, in the presence of the Father, Jesus Christ, an intercessor who is just.
                                                                      1 John 2:1-5

[Jesus] opened [the disciples'] minds to the understanding of the Scriptures. "You are witnesses of this."   Luke 24:35-48

The Risen Christ is present in this holy assembly.
With joyful confidence, then, let us pray:

- That our parish community may realize and celebrate
  the presence of the Risen Christ in our midst:
  let us pray to the Lord.

- That Pope N., Bishop N., Father N.,
  and all who serve the Church
  may be witnesses to the world of the Easter promise:
  let us pray to the Lord.

- That all nations and governments may seek, for all people,
  peace that is rooted in the justice and mercy of God:
  let us pray to the Lord.

- That parents and teachers
  may open the minds and hearts
  of their children and students
  to the compassion and justice of God:
  let us pray to the Lord.

- [That . . .:
  let us pray to the Lord.]

- That the lost, the troubled,
  and those who are enslaved by any form of abuse
  may find hope in the knowledge of Christ,
  our just intercessor before God:
  let us pray to the Lord.

- That the light of Christ's eternal peace
  may shine upon all our relatives and friends who have died
  [especially _____]:
  let us pray to the Lord.

- That God will hear the prayers
  we now offer in the silence of our hearts
  [Pause . . .]:
  let us pray to the Lord.

Father of life, hear our Easter prayer
that our re-creation in the image of the Risen Christ
may be complete,
and our rebirth in his new life
may be experienced in every moment you give us.
We ask this in the name of your Son,
our Lord and Risen Savior, Jesus Christ,
who lives and reigns with you for ever and ever.

Peter said to the leaders and elders: "In the power of [Jesus'] name this man stands before you perfectly sound." Acts 4:8-12

We know that when it comes to light we shall be like him. 1 John 3:1-2

"I am the good shepherd. I know my sheep and my sheep know me." John 10:11-18

Let us join our hearts and voices in prayer to the Lord,
our Father and Shepherd:

- For our parish community,
  that, together, we may live the gospel of the Good Shepherd
  in a spirit of peace and concern for one another:
  let us pray to the Lord.

- For Pope N., Bishop N., Father N.,
  and for all bishops, priests, deacons, and ministers,
  that they may lead the Church
  to the fulfillment of God's reign:
  let us pray to the Lord.

- For all states and nations,
  that they may enact laws and public policies
  which uphold the sacred dignity of every person
  as a child of God:
  let us pray to the Lord.

- For those who speak for the persecuted
  and who suffer with the oppressed,
  that Christ, who gives his life for his sheep,
  may be their power and strength:
  let us pray to the Lord.

- [For . . .,
  that . . .:
  let us pray to the Lord.]

- For the lost, the suffering,
  the addicted, and the abused,
  that they may hear the voice of the Good Shepherd
  in the help and compassion we extend to them:
  let us pray to the Lord.

- For the faithful who have died
  [especially _____],
  that the light of the Risen Christ
  may shine upon them for ever:
  let us pray to the Lord.

- For the prayers we now make in the silence of our hearts
  [Pause . . .]:
  let us pray to the Lord.

Father of love and Lord of life,
hear our Easter prayers.
May we be worthy to be your children
through our prayers and love
for all our brothers and sisters in the Risen Jesus,
who lives and reigns with you and the Holy Spirit
for ever and ever.

(Saul is welcomed into the community of disciples.)   Acts 9:26-31

Let us love in deed and in truth.   1 John 3:18-24

"I am the vine, you are the branches."   John 15:1-8

Confident that "God is with us
and that we will receive at his hands whatever we ask,"
let us pray:

- For our parish community,
  that we may be a rich and vibrant branch of Christ the Vine:
  let us pray to the Lord.

- For the bishops, priests, and ministers of our Church,
  that they may be agents of God's reconciling love:
  let us pray to the Lord.

- For all Christian Churches and communities,
  that they may be faithful to the love and peace of God
  both "in deed and in truth":
  let us pray to the Lord.

- For families and households,
  that they may know the joy of this Easter season
  in every season of every year:
  let us pray to the Lord.

- [For . . .,
  that . . .:
  let us pray to the Lord.]

- For the suffering, the persecuted, and the displaced,
  that the justice of God may be their hope
  and that our commitment to that justice
  may be their salvation:
  let us pray to the Lord.

- For the souls of our deceased relatives and friends
  [especially _____ *],*
  that they may live on in the life of the Risen Christ:
  let us pray to the Lord.

- For the prayers we now offer in the silence of our hearts
  [Pause . . .]:
  let us pray to the Lord.

Hear our Easter prayers, O Lord.
May your words forever be a part of us;
may your peace forever reign over us;
may your love forever unite us as your children.
We ask this in the name of your Son,
our Risen Savior, Jesus Christ,
who lives and reigns with you and the Holy Spirit
as the one God
for ever and ever.

(Peter addresses Cornelius' household) "The man of any nation who fears God and acts uprightly is acceptable to him." Acts 10:25-26, 34-35, 44-48

Love, then, consists in this: not that we have loved God, but that he has loved us.
1 John 4:7-10

"I call you friends since I have made known to you all that I heard from my Father."
John 15:9-17

The Risen Christ is present in this holy assembly.
With joyful confidence, then,
let us present our prayers to God in Jesus' name:

- For our Church and parish community,
  that our work and worship together
  may reflect the complete and unconditional love of God:
  let us pray to the Lord.

- For our bishops, priests, and deacons,
  for teachers, ministers, and preachers of the faith,
  that their generous service to God's people
  may bear much fruit:
  let us pray to the Lord.

- For the peoples and nations of the earth,
  that they may seek together the peace and justice of God:
  let us pray to the Lord.

- For the families and households of our community,
  that God's Spirit of love and unity
  may be poured out upon them:
  let us pray to the Lord.

- [For . . .,
  that . . .:
  let us pray to the Lord.]

- For the poor, the sick, and the suffering,
  that we may bring healing and hope into their lives
  through our faithful keeping of Jesus' commandment
  to love one another as he has loved us:
  let us pray to the Lord.

- For the faithful who have died
  [especially _____ *]*,
  that they may have eternal life through the Risen Christ:
  let us pray to the Lord.

- For the prayers we now offer in the silence of our hearts
  [Pause . . .]:
  let us pray to the Lord.

Make us be worthy, O God, to be your friends,
in our compassion and support for our friends here,
in our seeking what is right and acceptable in your eyes,
in our faithfulness to your commandment
   to love one another as you love us.
Grant these Easter prayers of ours
which we offer in the name of your Son, our Lord Jesus Christ,
who lives and reigns with you for ever and ever.

———————

ASCENSION OF THE LORD

See Year A.

(Matthias is chosen to be added to the Eleven.) Acts 1:15-17, 20-26

If we love one another, God dwells in us. 1 John 4:11-16

Jesus looked up to heaven and prayed: . . . "As you have sent me into the world, so I have sent them into the world." John 17:11-19

Let us now join our prayers
with Jesus' eternal prayer to the Father
for all of the human family:

- For our Church and parish community,
  that the God of love may always dwell in our midst:
  let us pray to the Lord.

- For the nations and peoples of the world,
  that they may welcome into their midst
  God's Word of reconciling love and peace:
  let us pray to the Lord.

- For those who claim the name of Christian,
  that they may accept, with the immediacy of Matthias,
  the call to be a disciple of the Risen Christ:
  let us pray to the Lord.

- For those to be ordained to the priesthood and diaconate,
  for seminarians, postulants, and novices,
  and for those preparing for lives of Christian service,
  that they may be consecrated in the Spirit of truth:
  let us pray to the Lord.

- For students,
  especially those graduating this spring,
  that their studies may lead them
  not only to competence and knowledge
  but to the wisdom and love of God:
  let us pray to the Lord.

- [For . . .,
  that . . .:
  let us pray to the Lord.]

- For the deceased members of our families and community
  [*especially* _____],
  that they may find, in the presence of Christ,
  light, happiness, and peace:
  let us pray to the Lord.

- For the prayers we now offer in the silence of our hearts
  [*Pause . . .*]:
  let us pray to the Lord.

Gracious God, hear the prayers of the people
your Son has gathered before you.
May every prayer we utter and every work we undertake
be to your glory
as we await the fulfillment of your promise
of eternal life in you
and he whom you have sent, Jesus Christ,
who lives and reigns with you for ever and ever.

PENTECOST

See Year A.

Moses said to the people: "Ask . . . from one end of the sky to the other:
Did anything so great ever happen before?" Deuteronomy 4:32-34, 39-40

[You received] a spirit of adoption through which we cry out, "Abba!"

Romans 8:14-17

"Go, therefore, and make disciples of all the nations. . . . Teach them to
carry out everything I have commanded you." Matthew 28:16-20

To the merciful and gracious Lord of all, let us pray:

- For our Church and parish community,
  that we may be always faithful to our calling
  to be the holy people of God:
  let us pray to the Lord.

- For all who serve the Church as pastors and ministers,
  that they may lead us in carrying out
  all that Jesus has commanded us:
  let us pray to the Lord.

- For the nations and peoples of the world,
  that they may glorify the Creator
  through the responsible care and just sharing
  of the gifts of God's holy creation:
  let us pray to the Lord.

- For parents, guardians, teachers, and counselors,
  that, through their own examples of love and selflessness,
  they may help our sons and daughters
  grow in the wisdom and knowledge of God:
  let us pray to the Lord.

- [For . . .,
  that . . .:
  let us pray to the Lord.]

- For the sick, the suffering, and the dying,
  that they may know the life of the Risen Christ:
  let us pray to the Lord.

- For all our deceased relatives and friends
  [*especially* _____],
  that they may be heirs of the eternal life of God:
  let us pray to the Lord.

- For the prayers we now offer in the silence of our hearts
  [*Pause . . .*]:
  let us pray to the Lord.

Gracious God, we call out to you,
not as a mysterious, cosmic riddle,
but as you have made yourself known to us:
    the God of compassion and love,
    the God who redeems us and restores us to life,
    the God who lives in us and through us.
Help us to love others as you love us,
without condition, without limit.
We make these prayers to you,
the Father, Son, and Spirit,
who lives and reigns for ever and ever.

"This is the blood of the covenant which the Lord has made with you in accordance with all these words of his."   Exodus 24:3-8

Christ came as high priest [and] . . . with his own blood . . . achieved eternal redemption.   Hebrews 9:11-15

"This is my blood, the blood of the covenant, to be poured out on behalf of many."   Mark 14:12-16, 22-26

Before we bring our gifts to the altar
for the blessing and breaking of bread,
let us ask God's blessings upon all people:

- That, in our prayer and work together,
  our Church and parish community may be faithful
  to our new covenant with God
  sealed in the Body and Blood of Christ Jesus:
  let us pray to the Lord.

- That those who serve in the ordained ministries of our Church
  may imitate, in their lives of service,
  the love of Christ, the Eternal High Priest:
  let us pray to the Lord.

- That all nations and peoples
  may "heed" God's word of justice and peace:
  let us pray to the Lord.

- That the Body and Blood of Christ, shed for all humanity,
  be the source of unity and reconciliation
  among all who claim the name of "Christian":
  let us pray to the Lord.

- [That . . .:
  let us pray to the Lord.]

- That the peace and unity we experience at this table
  may be translated into works of compassion and mercy
  for the poor and suffering members of Christ's body:
  let us pray to the Lord.

- That our deceased relatives and friends
  [especially _____]
  may receive the "promised eternal inheritance"
  of the life of God:
  let us pray to the Lord.

- That the living God will hear the prayers
  we now offer in the silence of our hearts
  [Pause . . .]:
  let us pray to the Lord.

Gracious Father, Giver and Nurturer of all life,
hear our prayers.
May the bread and wine of the Eucharist
make us bread for one another and for all,
that we might become ministers of your life and love
to our hurting world.
We ask this in the name of Jesus, the Bread of Life.

"Speak, for your servant is listening." 1 Samuel 3:3-10, 19

Your body is a temple of the Holy Spirit. 1 Corinthians 6:13-15, 17-20

The first thing [Andrew] did was seek out his brother Simon and tell him,
"We have found the Messiah!" John 1:35-42

To God, the Giver of all life and the Lord of peace,
let us pray:

- That our parish community may respond with open hearts
  to Christ's call to be his disciples:
  let us pray to the Lord.

- That the pastors and teachers of our Church,
  like Samuel and John the Baptizer,
  may proclaim, with courage and conviction,
  the presence of the Lamb of God among us:
  let us pray to the Lord.

- That society and public policies
  may uphold the dignity of every person
  as a temple of God's Spirit:
  let us pray to the Lord.

- That children and young people
  may hear the voice of God
  calling them to lives of joyful service to others:
  let us pray to the Lord.

- [That . . .:
  let us pray to the Lord.]

- That the sick and suffering,
  especially the victims of physical and sexual abuse,
  may be assured
  of our complete and unconditional help and support:
  let us pray to the Lord.

- That the souls of our deceased relatives and friends
  [especially _____]
  may be raised up by God to the life of the Resurrection:
  let us pray to the Lord.

- That the God of mercy will hear the prayers
  we now speak in the silence of our hearts
  [Pause . . .]:
  let us pray to the Lord.

Father, hear our prayers.
May we give voice to the presence of your Son,
the Lamb of God,
who is in our midst,
by seeking his peace and justice
in our time and place.
In his name, we pray.

(The Lord sends Jonah to proclaim a message of repentance to Nineveh.)

Jonah 3:1-5, 10

The world as we know it is passing away.   1 Corinthians 7:29-31

Jesus appeared in Galilee proclaiming God's good news:
". . . The reign of God is at hand."   Mark 1:14-20

With joy in the good news of the Father proclaimed by Christ Jesus,
let us come before our God in prayer:

- That our parish community may proclaim,
  in our work and worship together,
  the reign of God:
  let us pray to the Lord.

- That our Church may be a place
  of welcome and refuge for all people:
  let us pray to the Lord.

- That our bishops, priests, pastors, and ministers
  may proclaim the gospel with the perseverance of Jonah
  and the commitment of Peter, James, and John:
  let us pray to the Lord.

- That the world's governments and peoples may work together
  to insure the just and responsible use
  of the gifts of the earth:
  let us pray to the Lord.

- [That . . .:
  let us pray to the Lord.]

- That the grieving, the bitter, the troubled, and the lost
  may build new lives in the hope proclaimed by Christ:
  let us pray to the Lord.

- That our deceased relatives and friends
  [especially _____]
  may rejoice forever in the fulfillment of the reign of God:
  let us pray to the Lord.

- That God will hear the prayers
  we now speak in the silence of our hearts
  [Pause . . .]:
  let us pray to the Lord.

God of timelessness, Lord of history, hear our prayers.
Help us to realize that your gift of time
is not the end or limit of this life
but the pathway to the complete and perfect life
of the Risen One,
in whose name we offer these prayers.

"The Lord said . . ., 'I will raise up for them a prophet like [Moses] and will put my words into his mouth.'"   Deuteronomy 18:15-20

Devote yourselves entirely to the Lord.   1 Corinthians 7:32-35

(Jesus calls an unclean spirit out of a man at Capernaum.) "He gives orders to unclean spirits and they obey him!"   Mark 1:21-28

To God, the Source of life and Author of holiness, let us pray:

- For our Church and parish community,
  that we may be constantly attentive to the voice of God:
  let us pray to the Lord.

- For the bishops, priests and ministers of the Church,
  that they may truly speak the "words" of God:
  let us pray to the Lord.

- For the leaders of nations and officers of governments,
  that they may lead others
  by the authority of their own dedication and commitment
  to the justice and wisdom of God:
  let us pray to the Lord.

- For families and households,
  that God's Spirit of love may dwell in their midst:
  let us pray to the Lord.

- [For . . .,
  that . . .:
  let us pray to the Lord.]

- For the sick, the suffering, the troubled, and the dying,
  that they may know, in their anguish,
  the presence of Christ the Healer:
  let us pray to the Lord.

- For all who have died in the peace of Christ
  [especially _____],
  that they may live anew in the light and mercy of God:
  let us pray to the Lord.

- For the prayers we now make in the silence of our hearts
  [Pause . . .]:
  let us pray to the Lord.

Create us anew, O God,
in the life of the Holy One you sent to redeem us.
Cast out of our hearts and minds
the "unclean spirits" of hatred, prejudice, and greed
that lead us away from you,
and instill within us your Spirit of compassion and mercy.
Grant these prayers we make to you
in the name of your Son, our Lord and Savior, Jesus Christ.

"My life is like the wind; I shall not see happiness again."   Job 7:1-4, 6-7

To the weak I became a weak person with a view to winning the weak.
                                                    1 Corinthians 9:16-19, 22-23

Those whom [Jesus] cured, who were variously afflicted, were many,
and so were the demons he expelled.   Mark 1:29-39

Let us now join our hearts and voices in prayer for our human family:

- For our Church and parish,
  that we may be a source of healing and reconciliation
  for our community:
  let us pray to the Lord.

- For Pope N., Bishop N., Father N.,
  and for the bishops, priests, and ministers of our Church,
  that they may proclaim to the world
  the gospel of hope and reconciliation:
  let us pray to the Lord.

- For our President and the leaders of the world's nations,
  that the Spirit of God will inspire them
  to work for peace and justice among all peoples:
  let us pray to the Lord.

- [For . . .,
  that . . .:
  let us pray to the Lord.]

- For the victims of physical, mental, and substance abuse,
  that the love of God may expel from their lives
  the "demons" of pain, fear, and despair:
  let us pray to the Lord.

- For the sick, the suffering, and the dying,
  that Jesus the Healer may take their hands
  and raise them up to health and wholeness:
  let us pray to the Lord.

- For our deceased relatives and friends
  [especially _____ *],*
  that they may realize the hope of the gospel:
  let us pray to the Lord.

- For the prayers we now offer in the silence of our hearts
  [Pause . . .]:
  let us pray to the Lord.

O Lord, you have walked among us;
you know our pain and our brokenness.
May these prayers we offer be the beginning
of the mending of our relationships with one another
and the healing of our hearts in your hope and peace.
In Jesus' name, we pray.

"[The leper] shall dwell apart, making his abode outside the camp."

Leviticus 13:1-2, 44-46

Whatever you do—you should do all for the glory of God. 1 Corinthians 10:31–11:1

Moved with pity, Jesus stretched out his hand, touched [the leper], and said:
". . . Be cured." Mark 1:40-45

Let us offer our prayers to God, the Giver of life,
in the name of Jesus, the Healer and Restorer of life:

- That thanksgiving and gratitude to God
  may be the center of our parish's life together:
  let us pray to the Lord.

- That our bishops, priests, deacons, ministers, and teachers
  may be imitators of Christ, the Servant of God:
  let us pray to the Lord.

- That those considered lepers by society
  may be welcomed and honored in our midst:
  let us pray to the Lord.

- That physicians, medical personnel, and therapists
  may care for their patients
  with the compassion of Jesus:
  let us pray to the Lord.

- [That . . .:
  let us pray to the Lord.]

- That the sick and dying
  may be touched by the healing presence of Christ:
  let us pray to the Lord.

- That the faithful who have died
  [especially _____]
  may be reborn in the life of the Risen Christ:
  let us pray to the Lord.

- That the God of graciousness will hear the prayers
  we now offer in the silence of our hearts
  [Pause . . .]:
  let us pray to the Lord.

Hear our prayers, O God, for all the family of humankind.
Mend our broken relationships with one another;
heal us of the leprosy of selfishness and injustice;
make us clean and whole in your love and compassion.
We offer these prayers in the name of Jesus, the healing Christ.

SEVENTH SUNDAY OF THE YEAR   *YEAR B*

See, I am doing something new! Now it springs forth, do you not perceive it?
                                             Isaiah 43:18-19, 21-22, 24-25

Jesus Christ . . . was never anything but "yes."   2 Corinthians 1:18-22

*The four began to open up the roof. . . . They let down the mat on which the
paralytic was lying.*   Mark 2:1-12

With one heart and one voice,
let us present our prayers to God, the Lord of hope:

- That our Church and parish community
  may seek the mercy and love of God in all things:
  let us pray to the Lord.

- That Pope N., Bishop N., Father N.,
  and all who serve the Church
  may announce with joy and dedication
  God's word of forgiveness and reconciliation:
  let us pray to the Lord.

- That God's way of peace and justice
  may be the path traveled by all peoples and nations:
  let us pray to the Lord.

- [That . . .:
  let us pray to the Lord.]

- That we may imitate the friends of the paralyzed man
  in serving the sick, the poor, and the needy among us:
  let us pray to the Lord.

- That those on the margins of society—
  whose pain and anguish are ignored—
  may find, among us, a place of acceptance and support:
  let us pray to the Lord.

- That those who have died in the peace of Christ
  [*especially* _____]
  may find, in God's holy presence,
  light, happiness, and peace:
  let us pray to the Lord.

- That God will hear the prayers
  we now make in the silence of our hearts
  [Pause . . .]:
  let us pray to the Lord.

O God, hear the prayers of the people
who have placed their hope in you.
With a perfect and complete "yes,"
may we respond to your invitation
to make our lives "new"
in your love, compassion, and forgiveness.
In Jesus' name, we pray.

I will espouse you in right and in justice, in love and in mercy. Hosea 2:16, 17, 21-22

You are a letter of Christ . . . a letter written not with ink but by the Spirit of the living God. 2 Corinthians 3:1-6

"How can the guests at a wedding fast as long as the groom is still among them?"
Mark 2:18-22

To the Lord of kindness and mercy, let us pray:

- For our Church and parish community,
  that our work and worship together
  may celebrate the presence of Christ in our midst:
  let us pray to the Lord.

- For those who teach and proclaim the gospel,
  that their lives may be "letters" of God's Word,
  "known and read" by those they serve:
  let us pray to the Lord.

- For the nations of the world,
  that they may find new ways
  to foster justice and mercy among all peoples:
  let us pray to the Lord.

- For married couples and their families,
  that they may live their sacrament of Christ's love
  every day of their life together:
  let us pray to the Lord.

- [For . . .,
  that . . .:
  let us pray to the Lord.]

- For the poor, the neglected, and the abused,
  that we may give thanks for God's kindness to us
  by the kindness we extend to them:
  let us pray to the Lord.

- For our deceased relatives and friends
  [especially _____ *],*
  that God will welcome them
  to the eternal wedding feast of the Son:
  let us pray to the Lord.

- For the prayers we now offer in the silence of our hearts
  [Pause . . .]:
  let us pray to the Lord.

Loving Father, hear the prayers of the people
you have called to be your own.
May your Word of peace be written on our hearts
that our very lives may speak that Word
to a world longing to hear it.
We offer these prayers in the name of Jesus,
our Lord and Redeemer.

The seventh day is the sabbath of the Lord, your God.   Deuteronomy 5:12-15

God . . . has shone in our hearts, that we in turn might make known the glory of God shining in the face of Christ.   2 Corinthians 4:6-11

"The sabbath was made for man, not man for the sabbath."   Mark 2:23–3:6

To the Lord of the Sabbath and God of all seasons, let us pray:

- That we may make known the glory of God to all people
  through our life together as a Church and parish community:
  let us pray to the Lord.

- That our Church's pastors and ministers may proclaim,
  not condemnation or fear of God,
  but reconciliation and hope in God:
  let us pray to the Lord.

- That justice, integrity,
  and respect for the sacred dignity
  of every man, woman, and child
  may govern all our labors, endeavors, and relationships:
  let us pray to the Lord.

- [That . . .:
  let us pray to the Lord.]

- That those who are enslaved
  by persecution, poverty, or substance abuse
  may find liberation in the life and love of God:
  let us pray to the Lord.

- That the sick, the suffering, and the dying
  may be restored to health by the grace of the healing Jesus:
  let us pray to the Lord.

- That the Risen Christ will welcome into the house of God
  the souls of our deceased relatives and friends
  [especially _____]:
  let us pray to the Lord.

- That God our Savior and Protector will hear the prayers
  we now offer in the silence of our hearts
  [Pause . . .]:
  let us pray to the Lord.

Hear our prayers, O God, for all your holy people.
Open our hearts and minds to your Word made flesh
that we may make every day holy
as we await the dawning of your eternal day.
We make these prayers to you in the name of Jesus, our Light.

"I will put enmity between you and the woman, and between your offspring and hers."

Genesis 3:9-15

When the earthly tent in which we dwell is destroyed we have a dwelling provided for us by God.

1 Corinthians 4:13–5:1

"Whoever does the will of God is brother and sister and mother to me." Mark 3:20-35

To the God of kindness and forgiveness,
to the Father who redeems us through the Son,
let us confidently offer our prayers:

- That our Church and parish may be a place
  of forgiveness and reconciliation for all:
  let us pray to the Lord.

- That those who bring the good news of Christ to others
  through the ministries of teaching and healing
  may be received with welcome and joy:
  let us pray to the Lord.

- That the nations and peoples of the world may be united
  in their common pursuit of God's justice and peace:
  let us pray to the Lord.

- That families in crisis
  may find new joy and love in their life together
  through the healing presence of Christ:
  let us pray to the Lord.

- [That . . .:
  let us pray to the Lord.]

- That those mired in grief, despair, or addiction
  may, with our help and support,
  be raised up to joy, purpose, and hope:
  let us pray to the Lord.

- That those who have died in the peace of Christ
  [especially _____]
  may live forever in the dwelling place of God:
  let us pray to the Lord.

- That God will hear the prayers we now offer
  in the silence of our hearts
  [Pause . . .]:
  let us pray to the Lord.

O Lord, may the prayers we offer with one voice
make us one in heart and spirit as well.
Grant these prayers which we make to you
in the name of Christ Jesus, the Lord.

I, too, will tear off a tender shoot from the crest of the cedar . . . and plant it on a high and lofty mountain. Ezekiel 17:22-24

We walk by faith, not by sight. 2 Corinthians 5:6-10

"The reign of God . . . is like a mustard seed." Mark 4:26-34

To the God who lifts up the lowly, exalts the humble,
and blesses the poor with every good thing,
let us pray:

- For our Church and parish community,
  that our work and worship together
  may proclaim the kindness and faithfulness of our God:
  let us pray to the Lord.

- For those who serve our Church as pastors and teachers,
  that, through their ministries,
  the Word of God may take root in our lives:
  let us pray to the Lord.

- For those in government and public service,
  that, in all laws and public policies,
  they may seek to uphold
  the sacred dignity of every man, woman, and child:
  let us pray to the Lord.

- For all farmers and food producers,
  that God will bless their labors
  with a bountiful harvest for the benefit of all:
  let us pray to the Lord.

- [For . . .,
  that . . .:
  let us pray to the Lord.]

- For those who have dedicated themselves
  to the service of the poor and the oppressed,
  that their efforts may reap
  an abundant harvest of compassion and justice:
  let us pray to the Lord.

- For our deceased relatives and friends
  [especially _____ *],*
  that they may "flourish [forever] in the house of the Lord":
  let us pray to the Lord.

- For the prayers we now offer in the silence of our hearts
  [Pause . . .]:
  let us pray to the Lord.

Accept the gift of our prayers, O Lord,
which we offer for every member of our human family.
Like the crest of the cedar tree,
　　may we welcome all who come to us in need;
like the harvested seed,
　　may we grow in love and faith;
like the mustard seed,
　　may we praise you in even the smallest act
　　of kindness and joy.
We ask these things in the name
of our Lord and Teacher, Jesus Christ.

Who shut within doors the sea, when it burst forth from the womb; . . . .

Job 38:1, 8-11

If anyone is in Christ, he is a new creation. 2 Corinthians 5:14-17

Jesus . . . rebuked the wind and said to the sea: "Quiet! Be still!" Mark 4:35-41

Wondrous are all God's works of creation;
unfathomable is the depth of God's love for us.
In joyful hope, then, let us offer our prayers
to God, our Creator and Father:

- That our Church and parish community
  may be a place of welcome and safety
  for those who are afraid, lost, or alone:
  let us pray to the Lord.

- That the bishops, priests, and ministers of our Church
  may be "impelled" by the love of Christ
  to serve God's holy people
  with selflessness and compassion:
  let us pray to the Lord.

- That our nation, in its foreign policies and affairs,
  may be brother and sister to all the nations of the world:
  let us pray to the Lord.

- That we may give thanks to the Creator
  for the gift of the seas and the blessings of the earth
  by our just and responsible stewardship of the environment:
  let us pray to the Lord.

- [That . . .:
  let us pray to the Lord.]

- That we may calm the storms of fear, greed, and bigotry
  by our compassion, understanding, and support of those in need:
  let us pray to the Lord.

- That the faithful who have died
  [*especially* _____]
  may become a new creation in the Risen One:
  let us pray to the Lord.

- That God will hear the prayers
  we now speak in the silence of our hearts
  [*Pause . . .*]:
  let us pray to the Lord.

Gracious God, bless us with the wisdom, patience, and grace
to feel your presence amid the winds of despair and fear,
to hear your voice amid the roar of anger and mistrust,
to see your light in the darkness of prejudice and confusion.
We ask these things in the name of Jesus, the Lord.

God did not . . . rejoice in the destruction of the living. He fashioned all things that
they might have being. Wisdom 1:13-15; 2:23-24

For your sake [Jesus] made himself poor though he was rich,
so that you might become rich by his poverty. 2 Corinthians 8:7, 9, 13-15

(Jesus cures the daughter of Jairus.) Mark 5:21-43

In gratitude for what has been,
in hope for what will be,
let us offer our prayers to the God of life and joy:

- For our Church and parish,
  that we may be a community rich in the love of Christ:
  let us pray to the Lord.

- For Pope N., Bishop N., Father N.,
  and the bishops, priests, and deacons of our Church,
  that their ministries may touch the people they serve
  with compassion and understanding:
  let us pray to the Lord.

- For the nations and peoples of the world,
  that they may recognize, respect, and affirm
  the dignity of every person made in the very image of God:
  let us pray to the Lord.

- For all parents and guardians,
  that, like Jairus,
  they may seek the love and kindness of God
  for their children:
  let us pray to the Lord.

- [For . . .,
  that . . .:
  let us pray to the Lord.]

- For those who mourn and grieve,
  for families divided,
  for those consumed by despair and fear,
  that the love of God may transform
  their "mourning into dancing":
  let us pray to the Lord.

- For the faithful who have died
  [especially _____],
  that they may rise to the new life of the Risen Christ:
  let us pray to the Lord.

- For the prayers we now make in the silence of our hearts
  [Pause . . .]:
  let us pray to the Lord.

Lord of all hopefulness, Author of all goodness,
hear our prayers.
Do not let us surrender our hope to fear,
but may your Spirit inspire us
to trust always in what is right and good.
In Jesus' name, we pray.

Spirit entered into me [and said] . . . Son of man, I am sending you to the
Israelites. . . . They shall know that a prophet has been among them. Ezekiel 2:2-5

I willingly boast of my weakness . . ., that the power of Christ may rest upon me.
2 Corinthians 12:7-10

"What kind of wisdom is he endowed with? . . . Isn't this the carpenter,
the son of Mary?" Mark 6:1-6

Let us lift up our hearts and voices to the Lord in prayer
for all members of the human family:

- That the Spirit may enter into us,
  making of our Church and parish
  a community of compassion and forgiveness:
  let us pray to the Lord.

- That Pope N., Bishop N., Father N.,
  and our Church's bishops, priests, and ministers
  may be effective prophets
  of the justice and mercy of God:
  let us pray to the Lord.

- That President N., Governor N.,
  and the leaders of nations, states, and cities
  may lead their peoples with the authority
  born of wisdom and selflessness:
  let us pray to the Lord.

- That God's Spirit of peace and love
  may dwell within all families and households:
  let us pray to the Lord.

- [That . . .:
  let us pray to the Lord.]

- That the sick and the dying,
  the powerless and the addicted,
  may be restored to health and hope:
  let us pray to the Lord.

- That our deceased relatives and friends
  [especially _____]
  may be reborn in the new life of the Risen Christ:
  let us pray to the Lord.

- That God will hear the prayers we now offer
  in the silence of our hearts
  [Pause . . .]:
  let us pray to the Lord.

We come to you in hope, O Lord,
knowing that you will hear the prayers we ask in faith.
May your Spirit of wisdom and truth rest upon us always,
so that we may be prophets of your great love.
Grant these prayers we offer
in the name of your Son, Jesus Christ.

Amos answered Amaziah: ''I was no prophet. . . . I was a shepherd and dresser of
sycamores.''   Amos 7:12-15

When you heard the glad tidings of salvation, the word of truth, and believed in it,
you were sealed with the Holy Spirit.   Ephesians 1:3-14

Jesus summoned the Twelve and began to send them out two by two,
giving them authority over unclean spirits.   Mark 6:7-13

Let us now join our hearts and voices in prayer
for all who journey with us to the kingdom of God:

- That the grace of God may bind our Church and parish
  into a company of faithful disciples of Jesus:
  let us pray to the Lord.

- That our bishops, priests, and teachers
  may prophesy to all people
  ''the glad tidings of salvation'':
  let us pray to the Lord.

- That the peoples and nations of the world
  may work together to cast out of the human family
  hunger, materialism, prejudice, and injustice:
  let us pray to the Lord.

- That we may hear the voices of the prophets among us
  who call us to transform our world
  and renew our hearts
  in ''the Word of truth'':
  let us pray to the Lord.

- [That . . .:
  let us pray to the Lord.]

- That the sick and dying,
  the poor and homeless,
  the addicted and lost,
  may find, in our help and compassion,
  the restoring love of Christ the Healer:
  let us pray to the Lord.

- That those who have died in the peace of Christ
  [*especially* _____]
  may inherit God's promise of life in the Resurrection:
  let us pray to the Lord.

- That God will hear the prayers
  we now offer in the silence of our hearts
  [*Pause . . .*]:
  let us pray to the Lord.

Hear our prayers, O Lord,
and be with us on our journey.
May your peace guide our steps
and hope light our way
as we journey through life
to the joy of your kingdom,
where you live and reign for ever and ever.

I myself will gather the remnant of my flock [and] . . . appoint shepherds for them . . . so that they need no longer fear and tremble. Jeremiah 23:1-6

It is [Christ] who is our peace, and who made the two of us one by breaking down the barrier of hostility that kept us apart. Ephesians 2:13-18

[Jesus] pitied [the crowd], for they were like sheep without a shepherd; and he began to teach them. Mark 6:30-34

Let us now lift our spirits and voices in prayer
to the Lord, our Shepherd and Teacher:

- For our Church and parish community,
  that we may be a gathering place
  for the "remnant" from all lands and peoples:
  let us pray to the Lord.

- For Pope N., Bishop N., and Father N.,
  for our bishops, priests, and ministers,
  and for all who serve the Church,
  that they may shepherd the people of God
  with faithfulness and compassion:
  let us pray to the Lord.

- For our President and governor
  and for all legislators and judges,
  that their government service
  may advance the causes of peace and justice:
  let us pray to the Lord.

- For families and households,
  that the barriers of anger and division may be broken down
  through understanding and forgiveness:
  let us pray to the Lord.

- [For . . .,
  that . . .:
  let us pray to the Lord.]

- For the poor, the oppressed, and the brokenhearted,
  that, through our compassionate help,
  their fear and anguish may be transformed into hope and joy:
  let us pray to the Lord.

- For our deceased relatives and friends
  [*especially* _____],
  that they may dwell forever in the house of God:
  let us pray to the Lord.

- For the prayers we now offer in the silence of our hearts
  [*Pause . . .*]:
  let us pray to the Lord.

Lord God, hear the prayers we offer to you
for our Church and our human family.
May our community become
    a place of prayer that refreshes and sustains us;
may our ministries
    be places where your love and justice are revealed;
may our table
    be a place of welcome and nourishment for all.
We make these prayers in the name of your Son, our Lord Jesus Christ.

(Elisha feeds the people with twenty barley loaves.) 2 Kings 4:42-44

There is one Lord, one faith, one baptism; one God and Father of all. Ephesians 4:1-6

Jesus then took the loaves of bread [and dried fish], gave thanks,
and passed them around to those reclining there. John 6:1-15

Before we celebrate the sacrament of the Bread of Life,
let us join our hearts in prayer for our human family:

- That we may willingly and joyfully share
  our bread with the poor and hungry:
  let us pray to the Lord.

- That Christian Churches and communities
  may celebrate their common identity
  in the "one Lord, one faith, one baptism":
  let us pray to the Lord.

- That families, tribes, peoples, and races
  may find unity, understanding, and trust
  in the "God and Father of all":
  let us pray to the Lord.

- That a spirit of justice and thanksgiving
  may guide the work of all farmers,
  food producers and transporters,
  economists and agriculturalists:
  let us pray to the Lord.

- [That . . .:
  let us pray to the Lord.]

- That the poor, the homeless, and the forgotten
  may find places of welcome at our tables:
  let us pray to the Lord.

- That those who have died in Christ
  [*especially* _____]
  may celebrate forever at the banquet of heaven:
  let us pray to the Lord.

- That God will hear the prayers
  we now offer in the silence of our hearts
  [Pause . . .]:
  let us pray to the Lord.

Gracious God, Giver of every harvest,
hear the prayers we make
as we gather around our Eucharistic table.
May the bread and wine of your Son's Body and Blood
make us bread of compassion and kindness
and wine of gladness and hope for one another.
We ask this in the name of Jesus, the Bread of Life.

The Lord said to Moses, "I will now rain down bread from heaven for you."
Exodus 16:2-4, 12-15

You must put on that new man created in God's image,
whose justice and holiness are born of truth.   *Ephesians 4:17, 20-24*

"You should not be working for perishable food but for food that remains
unto life eternal."   *John 6:24-35*

To the Lord, who feeds us with the Bread of Heaven,
let us pray:

- For our Church and parish community,
  that we may do "the work of God"
  in every dimension of our life together:
  let us pray to the Lord.

- For Pope N., Bishop N., Father N.,
  and all who serve and minister to our Church,
  that they may teach "justice and holiness . . . born of truth":
  let us pray to the Lord.

- For President N., Governor N.,
  and all legislators, judges, and government officials,
  that they may lead and serve with courage and selflessness:
  let us pray to the Lord.

- [For . . .,
  that . . .:
  let us pray to the Lord.]

- For those whose lives are in transition,
  for those who are coping with loss,
  illness, or hardship in their lives,
  that God will be with them on their journeys:
  let us pray to the Lord.

- For the poor, the hungry, and the homeless,
  that we may share with them
  the blessings God has rained down upon us:
  let us pray to the Lord.

- For all who have died in the peace of Christ
  [*especially* _____],
  that Christ will welcome them to the banquet of heaven:
  let us pray to the Lord.

- For the prayers we now offer in the silence of our hearts
  [*Pause . . .*]:
  let us pray to the Lord.

You have done great things for us, O Lord;
rejoicing in the many blessings you have given us,
we come to you with these prayers,
confident, in faith, that you will hear them.
In Jesus' name, we pray.

Strengthened by that food, [Elijah] walked forty days and forty nights to the mountain of God, Horeb. 1 Kings 19:4-8

Be imitators of God as his dear children. Ephesians 4:30–5:2

"The bread I will give is my flesh, for the life of the world." John 6:41-51

The goodness of God has been revealed to us in so many ways:
in the wonders of creation
and in creation's *re-creation* in the Risen Christ.
With confidence, then, let us pray:

- For our Church and parish family,
  that we may become a community
  of compassion and forgiveness:
  let us pray to the Lord.

- For Pope N., Bishop N., Father N.,
  and for all who serve the Church,
  that they may lead us in the way of love
  taught by Christ:
  let us pray to the Lord.

- For the nations and governments of the world,
  that, in their laws and public policies,
  they may uphold the sacred character and dignity
  of every member of the human family:
  let us pray to the Lord.

- For those who shelter the homeless,
  feed the hungry, and counsel the grieving and troubled,
  that God may teach us through their example:
  let us pray to the Lord.

- [For . . .,
  that . . .:
  let us pray to the Lord.]

- For those fighting to overcome illness or addiction,
  that Christ will be with them on their difficult journeys:
  let us pray to the Lord.

- For the faithful who have died
  [*especially* _____],
  that the everlasting life of the Risen Christ may be theirs:
  let us pray to the Lord.

- For the prayers we now offer in the silence of our hearts
  [*Pause . . .*]:
  let us pray to the Lord.

Bread of heaven, Spirit of life,
hear these prayers of ours.
As you have become bread for us,
    make us bread for one another;
as your Spirit enlivens us with your love and peace,
    make us be love and peace for one another.
We offer these prayers in the name of Jesus,
the Bread of Heaven, the Risen Christ.

Wisdom has built her house, . . . she has spread her table. Proverbs 9:1-6

Try to discern the will of the Lord. Ephesians 5:15-20

"He who feeds on my flesh . . . has life eternal,
and I will raise him up on the last day." John 6:51-58

God invites us to the banquet of wisdom and life.
With confidence, then, let us pray:

- That our prayer and work together
  as a Church and parish community
  may be songs of thanksgiving to our gracious God:
  let us pray to the Lord.

- That the ministers of our Church
  and the leaders of nations
  may draw courage and understanding
  from the table of God's holy wisdom:
  let us pray to the Lord.

- That teachers and their students may,
  in their studies and research,
  "discern the will of the Lord" in all things:
  let us pray to the Lord.

- [That . . .:
  let us pray to the Lord.]

- That those suffering from any form of addiction or abuse
  may rebuild their lives
  in the hope of God's wisdom:
  let us pray to the Lord.

- That the poor, the homeless, and the forgotten
  may be welcomed to our banquet tables:
  let us pray to the Lord.

- That the faithful who have died
  [especially _____]
  may be raised up by Christ to the life of the Father:
  let us pray to the Lord.

- That God will hear the prayers we now offer
  in the silence of our hearts
  [Pause . . .]:
  let us pray to the Lord.

O God,
in giving us your Son in the bread of the Eucharist,
you have made us into your own body,
one holy people bound by your love.
May these prayers we offer
and our work to make them come true
make us bread for all people
and family to one another.
In Jesus' name, we pray.

"As for me and my household, we will serve the Lord." Joshua 24:1-2, 15-17, 18

Wives should be submissive to their husbands as if to the Lord. . . .
Husbands, love your wives, as Christ loved the church. Ephesians 5:21-32

"The words I spoke to you are spirit and life." John 6:60-69

"Lord, to whom shall we go?
You have the words of eternal life."
With Peter's simple expression of faith
echoing in our hearts, let us pray:

- For our Church and parish community,
  that we may endure in our vocation
  to be God's holy people:
  let us pray to the Lord.

- For our bishops, priests, deacons, and ministers,
  that they may speak Jesus' words of spirit and life:
  let us pray to the Lord.

- For married couples,
  that the love of Christ
  may be the center of their life together:
  let us pray to the Lord.

- [For . . .,
  that . . .:
  let us pray to the Lord.]

- For those whose lives are in turmoil,
  for families in crisis,
  that the Spirit of God may instill in them renewed hope
  and lead them to fulfillment and purpose:
  let us pray to the Lord.

- For the sick, the suffering, and the dying,
  that, in their pain and anguish,
  Christ may be present to them
  in our compassion and care:
  let us pray to the Lord.

- For those who have died in Christ's peace
  [especially _____],
  that Jesus' promise of eternal life may be theirs:
  let us pray to the Lord.

- For the prayers we now offer in the silence of our hearts
  [Pause . . .]:
  let us pray to the Lord.

Gracious God, hear our prayers.
Do not let us be discouraged
by the crosses of our lives,
but let us always carry on in hope,
in the certainty of your Son's words of spirit and life.
In his name, we pray.

*"Now, Israel, hear the statutes and decrees which I am teaching you to observe,
that you may live."*   Deuteronomy 4:1-2, 6-8

Humbly welcome the word that has taken root in you.   James 1:17-18, 21-22, 27

"That which comes out of [a man], and only that, constitutes impurity."
Mark 7:1-8, 14-15, 21-23

Our God hears the stirrings of every human heart.
With confidence, then,
let us now lift up our hearts in prayer:

- That our parish's worship and work together
  may be a constant celebration of God's great love:
  let us pray to the Lord.

- That the laws and policies of all governments
  may honor the sacred character of every man, woman, and child
  as sons and daughters of God:
  let us pray to the Lord.

- That the new school year may be, for our children,
  a time of discovery and growth in the wisdom of God:
  let us pray to the Lord.

- That a commitment to justice
  and an awareness of social responsibility
  may guide all businesses and banking institutions
  in the conduct of their financial affairs:
  let us pray to the Lord.

- [That . . .:
  let us pray to the Lord.]

- That the generosity and compassion we extend
  to the poor, the hungry, and the homeless
  may be an offering of thanksgiving
  for God's many blessings to us:
  let us pray to the Lord.

- That the faithful who have died
  [*especially* _____]
  may share in the eternal life of the Risen Christ:
  let us pray to the Lord.

- That the Father will hear the prayers
  we now offer in the silence of our hearts
  [*Pause . . .*]:
  let us pray to the Lord.

May your Word of life and love
take root in our hearts, O God,
that these prayers we offer
may become a harvest of justice and peace.
In Jesus' name, we pray.

Be strong, fear not! Here is your God, he comes with vindication. Isaiah 35:4-7

Did not God choose those who are poor in the eyes of the world to be rich in faith and heirs of the kingdom? James 2:1-5

Jesus . . . said to [the deaf man], "Ephphatha!" Mark 7:31-37

"Ephphatha!"—Be opened!
With hearts and spirits opened to God's healing presence,
let us pray:

- For our Church and parish community,
  that our work and worship together
  may reflect the gospel of reconciliation and compassion:
  let us pray to the Lord.

- For the ministers of the Church
  and the leaders of nations,
  that they may proclaim the justice and peace of God
  without fear or compromise:
  let us pray to the Lord.

- For professors, scholars, researchers, and teachers,
  that they may enable society
  to recognize the hand of God
  sustaining life in all of creation:
  let us pray to the Lord.

- [For . . .,
  that . . .:
  let us pray to the Lord.]

- For the poor, the homeless, and the abused,
  that they may find a place of honor and welcome
  in our homes, parish, and community:
  let us pray to the Lord.

- For the sick and the suffering,
  for those whose lives are in crisis,
  for the lost and the despairing,
  that the love of Christ the Healer may open their lives
  to healing and wholeness:
  let us pray to the Lord.

- For our deceased relatives and friends
  [especially _____],
  that they may be heirs of the promised kingdom of God:
  let us pray to the Lord.

- For the prayers we now offer in the silence of our hearts
  [Pause . . .]:
  let us pray to the Lord.

Open our eyes and ears and hearts to your Spirit, O God,
that everything we do and every moment you give us
may speak of your loving presence in our world.
We offer our prayers in the name of your Son,
our Lord Jesus Christ.

The Lord God is my help, therefore I am not disgraced. Isaiah 50:4-9

What good is it to profess faith without practicing it? James 2:14-18

"If a man wishes to come after me, he must deny his very self, take up his cross, and follow in my steps." Mark 8:27-35

To the God of mercy and reconciliation,
let us lift up our hearts and voices in prayer:

- That every ministry of our parish
  may proclaim the Messiah's presence among us:
  let us pray to the Lord.

- That those who serve our Church
  as bishops, priests, pastors, and teachers
  may proclaim the gospel
  with courage, integrity, and perseverance:
  let us pray to the Lord.

- That the laws and public policies
  of the world's governments and nations
  may be dedicated to serving the common good:
  let us pray to the Lord.

- That those peoples and Churches
  who are persecuted for their faith and beliefs
  may persevere in the hope
  that the peace and justice of God will one day reign:
  let us pray to the Lord.

- [That . . .:
  let us pray to the Lord.]

- That the faith we profess may find expression
  in our compassionate care
  for the poor, the lost, and the forgotten:
  let us pray to the Lord.

- That those who have died in Christ's peace
  [especially _____]
  may walk forever in the presence of God:
  let us pray to the Lord.

- That God, our gracious Father, will hear the prayers
  we now offer in the silence of our hearts
  [Pause . . .]:
  let us pray to the Lord.

Gracious God, hear the prayers we lift up to you.
Give us the courage and generosity
to crucify our self-interests
and take up our crosses to follow Christ,
so that we may bring his new life and liberation to our world.
We offer these prayers in the name of Jesus,
the Messiah and Redeemer.

If the just one be the son of God, he will defend him and deliver him from the hand of his foes. Wisdom 2:12, 17-20

The harvest of justice is sown in peace for those who cultivate peace. James 3:16–4:3

"If anyone wishes to rank first, he must remain the last one of all and the servant of all. . . . Whoever welcomes a child such as this for my sake welcomes me."
Mark 9:30-37

As a community of peace and compassion,
let us offer our prayers to our merciful and loving God:

- That our Church and parish may seek, in all things,
  to become a community of reconciliation and forgiveness:
  let us pray to the Lord.

- That all peoples and nations may "cultivate peace"
  in order to reap "a harvest of justice":
  let us pray to the Lord.

- That our parish religious education teachers
  may guide and inspire our children
  in the wonders and wisdom of God:
  let us pray to the Lord.

- [That . . .:
  let us pray to the Lord.]

- That those who have dedicated themselves
  to the service of the poor and oppressed
  may be exalted as first in the reign of God:
  let us pray to the Lord.

- That we may hear,
  with openness of heart and generosity of spirit,
  the voices of those who cry out
  for mercy and justice:
  let us pray to the Lord.

- That God will raise up to new life
  those who have died in the peace of Christ
  [especially _____ *]:*
  let us pray to the Lord.

- That God will hear the prayers we now offer
  in the silence of our hearts
  [Pause . . .]:
  let us pray to the Lord.

Gracious Father, hear our prayers.
Enliven us with the Spirit of Christ the Servant,
that we may serve and honor you
by serving and honoring one another;
inspire us with the wonder of a child,
that we may seek with gratitude
the simple and humble ways of your justice and peace.
We ask these things in the name of your Son,
our Lord Jesus Christ.

The spirit came to rest on [Eldad, Medad, and the seventy], they prophesied.
Numbers 11:25-29

*Here, crying aloud, are the wages you withheld from the farmhands who
harvested your fields.* James 5:1-6

*"It would be better if anyone who leads astray one of these simple believers
were to be plunged in the sea."* Mark 9:38-43, 45, 47-48

Let us now offer our prayers to God,
the Father of justice and compassion:

- For our Church and parish community,
  that in our prayer and work together
  we may proclaim God's great love for all of humankind:
  let us pray to the Lord.

- For those who proclaim the gospel
  as teachers, writers, scholars, and preachers,
  that the Spirit of God may be revealed in their work:
  let us pray to the Lord.

- For the leaders of nations and the peoples of the world,
  that the Spirit of peace, understanding, and wisdom
  may come to rest upon them:
  let us pray to the Lord.

- For those who manage corporations and financial institutions,
  that they may conduct their businesses with justice
  and a commitment to the common good:
  let us pray to the Lord.

- [For . . .,
  that . . .:
  let us pray to the Lord.]

- For those who are suffering from the effects
  of physical, sexual, or substance abuse,
  that they may be healed and made whole
  through the compassionate care of family and friends:
  let us pray to the Lord.

- For those who have died in the peace of Christ
  [especially _____ *]*,
  that they may be welcomed into the company of the saints:
  let us pray to the Lord.

- For the prayers we now offer in the silence of our hearts
  [Pause . . .]:
  let us pray to the Lord.

Bestow your Spirit upon us, O Lord,
so that in all things we may act in Jesus' name:
to reach out to one another
without condition, without judgment, without bias,
without thought to the cost—
for no other reason than
that they are your sons and daughters.
Hear these prayers we offer for them and for us
in the name of your Son, our Lord Jesus Christ.

"It is not good for the man to be alone." Genesis 2:18-24

Jesus was made . . . lower than the angels, that through God's gracious will he might taste death for the sake of all. Hebrews 2:9-11

"They are no longer two but one flesh. Therefore let no one separate what God has joined." Mark 10:2-16

Let us now lift our hearts and voices in prayer to God
for all the human family:

- For our Church and parish community,
  that in our prayer and work together
  we may proclaim the reign of God:
  let us pray to the Lord.

- For the nations and peoples of the world,
  that all humanity may be bound by the love of God
  into a family of brothers and sisters:
  let us pray to the Lord.

- For married couples,
  that they may always find joy and fulfillment
  in the sacrament of their life together in Christ:
  let us pray to the Lord.

- For children and young people,
  that they may grow and learn in an environment
  of nurturing love and patient understanding:
  let us pray to the Lord.

- [For . . .,
  that . . .:
  let us pray to the Lord.]

- For those experiencing the pain and trauma
  of loss, separation, or divorce,
  that they may rebuild their lives
  with the compassionate support of family and friends:
  let us pray to the Lord.

- For our deceased relatives and friends
  [especially _____],
  that they may walk forever
  in the light and peace of God's presence:
  let us pray to the Lord.

- For the prayers we now offer in the silence of our hearts
  [Pause . . .]:
  let us pray to the Lord.

To you who are the Father of creation,
the Source of love and peace,
the Protector of the poor and lost,
we offer these prayers for all our brothers and sisters.
Hear and grant these prayers we offer
in the name of your Son, Jesus the Christ.

All gold, in view of [wisdom], is a little sand.   Wisdom 7:7-11

God's word . . . judges the reflections and thoughts of the heart.   Hebrews 4:12-13

"It is easier for a camel to pass through a needle's eye than for a rich man to enter the kingdom of God."   Mark 10:17-30

"With God all things are possible."
With confidence in Jesus' promise, then, let us pray:

- That we may seek to follow Christ totally and completely
  in every dimension of our life together
  as a Church and parish community:
  let us pray to the Lord.

- That the pastors, preachers, and teachers of our Church
  may proclaim the "living and effective" Word of God
  with compassion and understanding:
  let us pray to the Lord.

- That the nations and governments of the world
  may work together to provide all people
  with a just share of the earth's harvest:
  let us pray to the Lord.

- That all businesses and financial institutions
  may conduct their affairs with integrity
  and respect for the sacredness of every person:
  let us pray to the Lord.

- [That . . .:
  let us pray to the Lord.]

- That we may embrace the gospel spirit of poverty
  for the sake of the poor, the homeless, and the hungry:
  let us pray to the Lord.

- That all who have died in the peace of Christ
  [*especially* _____]
  may dwell forever in the house of God:
  let us pray to the Lord.

- That God will hear the prayers we now offer
  in the silence of our hearts
  [Pause . . .]:
  let us pray to the Lord.

Enliven us with your Spirit of love, O Lord,
so that we may seek your mercy and justice for all people;
bless us with the light of your wisdom,
so that we may follow Christ Jesus
to make these prayers a reality.
In Jesus' name, we pray.

Through his suffering, my servant shall justify many. Isaiah 53:10-11

Let us confidently approach the throne of grace to receive mercy and favor
and to find help in time of need. Hebrews 4:14-16

"The Son of Man has not come to be served but to serve—to give his life in
ransom for the many." Mark 10:35-45

To the Lord of kindness and hope, let us pray:

- That our Church and parish
  may be formed by the Spirit
  into a faithful community of disciples:
  let us pray to the Lord.

- That "the will of the Lord [may] be accomplished"
  through the teaching and example
  of our Church's bishops, priests, deacons, and ministers:
  let us pray to the Lord.

- That the leaders and rulers of nations
  may govern their people
  with justice, understanding, and a commitment to the common good:
  let us pray to the Lord.

- That those who are forced
  to drink from the cup of suffering and persecution
  may persevere in faith
  to experience one day the victory of Christ's resurrection:
  let us pray to the Lord.

- [That . . .:
  let us pray to the Lord.]

- That the sick, the suffering, and the dying
  may receive "mercy and favor" before the "throne of grace":
  let us pray to the Lord.

- That the souls of those who have died
  [*especially* _____]
  may share in the glory of the reign of the Risen Christ:
  let us pray to the Lord.

- That God will hear the prayers we now offer
  in the silence of our hearts
  [Pause . . .]:
  let us pray to the Lord.

Father, grant us the courage and perseverance
to be worthy disciples of your Son;
may we seek forgiveness rather than vengeance;
may we honor humility and selflessness
    as well as success and achievement;
may we insist on compassion and justice
    regardless of the cost.
Hear these prayers we offer, O God,
in the name of your Son,
our Lord and Redeemer, Jesus Christ.

I will gather [the remnant] from the ends of the world. Jeremiah 31:7-9

Every high priest is taken from among men and made their representative before God.
Hebrews 5:1-6

"Rabboni," the blind man said, "I want to see." Mark 10:46-52

Let us pray that God's light
may illuminate our minds and hearts
and guide us in God's peace:

- For our Church and parish family,
  that we may seek to follow Christ by becoming
  a community of compassion and reconciliation:
  let us pray to the Lord.

- For Pope N., Bishop N., Father N.,
  and for all who serve the Church,
  that they may gather us and unite us
  as God's holy people:
  let us pray to the Lord.

- For our President and governor,
  for our legislators and judges,
  and for all who serve us in government,
  that they may uphold and protect
  the sacred dignity of every person:
  let us pray to the Lord.

- [For . . .,
  that . . .:
  let us pray to the Lord.]

- For those who are mentally impaired or physically disabled,
  that we may be given the grace and wisdom
  to welcome them and enable them to use their gifts
  for the benefit of the entire human family:
  let us pray to the Lord.

- For those who are lost and troubled,
  who are mired in fear and despair,
  who feel abandoned by God,
  that, with our help and support,
  they may embrace the love and hope of the Father:
  let us pray to the Lord.

- For those who have died
  [especially _____],
  that they may one day awake and arise in the light of Christ:
  let us pray to the Lord.

- For the prayers we now offer in the silence of our hearts
  [Pause . . .]:
  let us pray to the Lord.

Lord of light, restore us with your vision of selfless love
so that we may make real in our lives
the prayers and hopes that you alone see
in the depths of our hearts.
Hear the prayers which we ask of you
in the name of Jesus, the healing Christ.

Fear the Lord, your God, and keep . . . all his statutes and commandments which I enjoin on you, and thus have a long life. Deuteronomy 6:2-6

Jesus, because he remains forever, has a priesthood which does not pass away.
Hebrews 7:23-28

" 'To love [the Lord your God] . . . is worth more than any burnt offering or sacrifice.' " Mark 12:28-34

To God, the Father of compassion and Author of love,
let us offer our prayers for all the human family:

- That the Spirit of love and compassion
  may breathe the life of God
  into every ministry of our Church and parish community:
  let us pray to the Lord.

- That those who serve the Church
  as bishops, priests, deacons, and ministers
  may seek to imitate the compassion and humility
  of Jesus Christ, the Eternal High Priest:
  let us pray to the Lord.

- That the nations and peoples of the world
  may grow and prosper in God's ways of peace and justice:
  let us pray to the Lord.

- That lawyers, teachers, and journalists
  may seek and reveal the depth of God's truth
  in every human endeavor:
  let us pray to the Lord.

- [That . . .:
  let us pray to the Lord.]

- That we may see in the faces of the poor,
  the abused, and the unwanted
  the face of the suffering Christ:
  let us pray to the Lord.

- That the faithful who have died
  [especially _____]
  may live anew in the reign of God:
  let us pray to the Lord.

- That God will hear the prayers
  we now offer in the silence of our hearts
  [Pause . . .]:
  let us pray to the Lord.

Accept, O gracious God,
the humble offering of our prayers
for all our human family.
May we praise you for your great love for us
by returning that love to one another
in humble and selfless compassion and service.
We offer these prayers to you in the name of your Son,
your Love incarnate, Jesus Christ.

(Elijah blesses the widow for her kindness with "the jar of flour that shall not go empty.")
1 Kings 17:10-16

Christ was offered up once to take away the sins of many. Hebrews 9:24-28

"They gave from their surplus wealth, but [the widow] gave from her want."
Mark 12:38-44

Let us now join our hearts and voices
in prayer to our heavenly Father
for all our brothers and sisters in Christ:

- That we may build our Church and parish
  into a community of disciples
  through our humble and compassionate service to one another:
  let us pray to the Lord.

- That our bishops, priests, deacons, and ministers
  may imitate the humility and selflessness
  of Christ, the Servant of God:
  let us pray to the Lord.

- That all nations and peoples,
  all Churches and communities,
  may be dedicated to the work of peace and justice
  and the elimination of oppression and persecution
  from our world:
  let us pray to the Lord.

- That we may seek out and treasure the insight and wisdom
  of the senior members and elders of our families and communities:
  let us pray to the Lord.

- [That . . .:
  let us pray to the Lord.]

- That, like the poor widow,
  we may respond to the plight of the hungry,
  the homeless, and the unwanted,
  not from our surplus, but from our want:
  let us pray to the Lord.

- That those who have died in the peace of Christ
  [especially _____ *]*
  may be welcomed by the angels and saints
  into the kingdom of God:
  let us pray to the Lord.

- That God will hear the prayers we now offer
  in the silence of our hearts
  [Pause . . .]:
  let us pray to the Lord.

May the prayers we offer, O God,
not be for greater things and talents to astound the world,
but for greater love and compassion to enrich the world.
Hear our prayers for the peace of our human family—
prayers we offer to you in the name of your Son,
our Lord Jesus Christ.

At that time your people shall escape, everyone who is found written in the book.
Daniel 12:1-3

Jesus offered one sacrifice for sins and took his seat forever at the right hand of God.
Hebrews 10:11-14, 18

"Learn a lesson from the fig tree. . . . The heavens and the earth will pass away,
but my words will not pass." Mark 13:24-32

To God, who is our life and our hope, let us pray:

- That our Church and parish community
  may be a living sign of hope in the reign of God:
  let us pray to the Lord.

- That the nations and peoples of the world
  may put aside mistrust, prejudice, and hatred,
  and be united under God, the Father of all:
  let us pray to the Lord.

- That those who fight and suffer for justice
  may shine like "the [stars] of the firmament,"
  inspiring us to follow them in their struggle:
  let us pray to the Lord.

- [That . . .:
  let us pray to the Lord.]

- That those who are experiencing
  traumatic change in their lives—
  due to separation, unemployment, illness, or abandonment—
  may continue their journeys in hope,
  always aware of the healing presence of Christ in their lives:
  let us pray to the Lord.

- That the hope and healing of Christ
  will illumine the days
  of the sick, the suffering, the recovering, and the dying:
  let us pray to the Lord.

- That all who have died in the peace of Christ
  [especially _____]
  may experience the fullness of joy in God's presence:
  let us pray to the Lord.

- That God will hear the prayers we now offer
  in the silence of our hearts
  [Pause . . .]:
  let us pray to the Lord.

Hear our prayers, O God,
you who are the beginning and end
of all things and seasons.
May we treasure the preciousness
of the time you have given us,
so that we may live our lives in joyful expectation
of the forever of your eternal reign.
In Jesus' name, we pray.

His dominion is an everlasting dominion that shall not be taken away.   Daniel 7:13-14

See, he comes amid the clouds! Every eye shall see him, even of those who pierced him.
Revelation 1:5-8

"My kingdom does not belong to this world."   John 18:33-37

In joyful hope, let us come together in prayer
before Jesus, our King and Redeemer:

- That our Church and parish community
  may be a faithful witness
  to the love and mercy of our heavenly Father:
  let us pray to the Lord.

- That Pope N., Bishop N., Father N.,
  and all who serve the Church
  may embrace Christ's priesthood
  of loving and humble service:
  let us pray to the Lord.

- That the nations and peoples of the world
  may serve one another
  in the justice and peace of God's reign:
  let us pray to the Lord.

- [That . . .:
  let us pray to the Lord.]

- That we may proclaim the great mystery of God's love
  through our compassion and charity
  to the poor, the homeless, and the abandoned:
  let us pray to the Lord.

- That the sick, the dying, and the recovering
  may be blessed by God with hope and "length of days":
  let us pray to the Lord.

- That the victorious Christ will gather
  into the kingdom of his Father
  the souls of all who have died
  [especially _____]:
  let us pray to the Lord.

- That God will hear the prayers we now offer
  in the silence of our hearts
  [Pause . . .]:
  let us pray to the Lord.

We praise you, O God,
you who are Lord of creation
and Ruler of all nations.
Hear the prayers we offer in joyful hope
until the coming of our Messiah and King,
our Lord Jesus Christ,
who lives and reigns with you and the Holy Spirit
as the one God,
for ever and ever.

YEAR C

I will raise up for David a just shoot.   Jeremiah 33:14-16

May [the Lord] strengthen your hearts, making them blameless and holy . . . at the coming of our Lord Jesus.   1 Thessalonians 3:12–4:2

[You] will see the Son of Man coming on a cloud with great power and glory.   Luke 21:25-28, 34-36

Let us begin this season of hope and expectation
with hearts and voices raised in prayer
to ''the Lord our justice'':

- That our parish community
  may ''overflow'' with the love of Christ
  for one another and for all:
  let us pray to the Lord.

- That all nations and peoples may dwell
  secure in the peace and justice of God:
  let us pray to the Lord.

- That this Advent season may be a time,
  not for mindless consumerism,
  but for the renewal and re-creation of human hearts:
  let us pray to the Lord.

- That families in crisis
  and those who are separated and estranged from one another
  may rediscover love and faithfulness
  in this season of light and hope:
  let us pray to the Lord.

- [That . . .:
  let us pray to the Lord.]

- That the sick and the dying
  may be strengthened by our prayer and compassion for them:
  let us pray to the Lord.

- That Christ will bring into his Father's presence
  the souls of all our deceased relatives and friends
  [especially _____]:
  let us pray to the Lord.

- That God will grant in kindness and mercy
  the prayers we now make in the silence of our hearts
  [Pause . . .]:
  let us pray to the Lord.

Come, O Lord, and redeem us.
Heal us with your peace,
teach us in your ways of justice and mercy,
and re-create us in your love.
We ask this in the name of your Son, our Lord Jesus Christ.

Jerusalem, take off your robe of mourning and misery. Baruch 5:1-9

May [you] be found rich in the harvest of justice. Philippians 1:4-6, 8-11

[John] went about the entire region of the Jordan proclaiming a baptism of repentance.
Luke 3:1-6

In joyful expectation of the day of Christ Jesus to come,
let us pray:

- That in our parish's prayer and work together
  we may create a highway for our God:
  let us pray to the Lord.

- That our bishops, priests, and deacons,
  and all who serve and minister to the Church
  may be heralds of God's presence among us:
  let us pray to the Lord.

- That those in government and public service
  may be instruments of the mercy and justice of God:
  let us pray to the Lord.

- That the Churches of Christendom
  may be "rich in the harvest of justice":
  let us pray to the Lord.

- That those who have been displaced from their homes
  by war, famine, disease, or disaster
  may return in joy and safety to their families:
  let us pray to the Lord.

- [That . . .:
  let us pray to the Lord.]

- That the poor, the struggling, and those who have lost hope
  may, through our compassionate help and support,
  remove their "robe of mourning and misery"
  and put on the hope and peace of the Messiah:
  let us pray to the Lord.

- That those who have died
  [especially _____]
  may rejoice forever in the city of God:
  let us pray to the Lord.

- That God, in mercy and peace, will hear the prayers
  we now make in the silence of our hearts
  [Pause . . .]:
  let us pray to the Lord.

Lord God, hear the prayers of your people
who anxiously await your coming.
Help us to straighten the crooked roads of our lives
so that we might create a highway
for you to enter our homes and hearts
with the peace of Christ Jesus, your Son,
in whose name we offer you these prayers.

The Lord, your God, is in your midst.	Zephaniah 3:14-18
Rejoice in the Lord always!	Philippians 4:4-7
The crowds asked John, "What ought we to do?"	Luke 3:10-18

Let us now offer our prayers in joyful hope to the Lord,
who comes to heal us and save us:

- That, in our ministries of prayer and charity,
  our Church and parish may reveal
  the joy of God's presence among us:
  let us pray to the Lord.

- That all nations and peoples may confidently and courageously
  seek the peace of God in every human endeavor:
  let us pray to the Lord.

- That generosity and compassion
  may be the center of our Advent preparation
  for the coming of Christ:
  let us pray to the Lord.

- That this Christmas season may be a time
  of healing and reconciliation
  with those from whom we are estranged and separated:
  let us pray to the Lord.

- That we might bring the life of Christ
  to the deserts of despair
  and the parched lands of hopelessness
  within our homes and communities:
  let us pray to the Lord.

- [That . . .:
  let us pray to the Lord.]

- That all who have died in the peace of Christ
  [especially _____]
  may be gathered into the eternal dwelling place of God:
  let us pray to the Lord.

- For the prayers we now make in the silence of our hearts
  [Pause . . .]:
    let us pray to the Lord.

Gracious God, hear our prayers.
May your Spirit come upon us
to transform our lives and our world
    from barrenness to harvest,
    from sickness to wholeness,
    from division to completeness,
    from death to life.
We ask this in the name of Jesus, Emmanuel.

From you [Bethlehem] shall come forth one who is to be ruler in Israel.   Micah 5:1-4

(A new covenant is established in Jesus Christ.)   Hebrews 10:5-10

(Elizabeth's greeting to Mary)
"Blessed are you among women and blessed is the fruit of your womb."   Luke 1:39-45

In joyful anticipation of the Lord's coming at Christmas,
let us join our hearts and voices in prayer:

- For our Church and parish community,
  that, like the almost unseen village of Bethlehem,
  we may reflect, in our life together,
  the light of God's love:
  let us pray to the Lord.

- For the nations and peoples of the world,
  that the reign of God's justice and mercy
  may reach to the ends of the earth:
  let us pray to the Lord.

- For all parents and guardians of children,
  that they may see in Mary and Elizabeth
  models of loving patience and selfless devotion
  to children and family:
  let us pray to the Lord.

- For those who do not celebrate Christ's birth,
  that they, too, may know the joy and peace of God's reign:
  let us pray to the Lord.

- For our Jewish neighbors and friends,
  our ancestors in the faith,
  that God will continue to bless them
  with happiness and peace:
  let us pray to the Lord.

- [For . . .,
  that . . .:
  let us pray to the Lord.]

- For those who have died in the peace of Christ
  [especially _____ *]*,
  that the new life of the Messiah may be theirs:
  let us pray to the Lord.

- For the prayers we now make in the silence of our hearts
  [Pause . . .]:
  let us pray to the Lord.

O Lord, our Shepherd and Guide,
come and shatter the darkness of our world
with the light of your love.
May these prayers we offer
and our work to bring them to fulfillment
bring the light and peace of the Messiah
into our own time and place.
We ask this in the name of our hope, Jesus, the Christ.

————————

The Sundays and Feasts of
THE CHRISTMAS SEASON

See Year A.

ASH WEDNESDAY

See Year A.

(Moses and Israel bring before the Lord the first fruits of the land the Lord gave them.)
Deuteronomy 26:4-10

All have the same Lord, [who is] rich in mercy. Romans 10:8-13

[Jesus] was led by the Spirit into the desert for forty days where he was tempted by the devil.
Luke 4:1-13

To the Lord of compassion and mercy,
let us offer our prayers:

- That this Lenten season may be a time of reconciliation
  within our families, our parish, and our community:
  let us pray to the Lord.

- That those who govern nations and human destinies
  may be committed to the justice and mercy of God,
  working unceasingly for the alleviation
  of hunger and misery from our world:
  let us pray to the Lord.

- That, in making moral and ethical choices,
  we may not bow before money, power, and prestige,
  but seek the justice and mercy of God in all things:
  let us pray to the Lord.

- That works of charity, generosity, and compassion
  may be the "first fruits" we offer to God
  during this holy season:
  let us pray to the Lord.

- [That . . .:
  let us pray to the Lord.]

- That the God of mercy and compassion
  will be the refuge and hope of the sick and dying:
  let us pray to the Lord.

- That all who have died
  [especially _____ *]*
  and those who will return to God during this Lenten season
  may experience the eternal life of the victorious Christ:
  let us pray to the Lord.

- That God will hear the prayers we now offer
  in the silence of our hearts
  [Pause . . .]:
  let us pray to the Lord.

Hear the prayers we offer you, O Lord.
During these holy days of Lent,
may we dedicate ourselves to the work
of making these prayers a reality.
We ask these things of you
in the name of Jesus, our Redeemer.

(God's covenant with Abraham) Genesis 15:5-12, 17-18

[Christ] will give new form to this lowly body of ours. Philippians 3:17–4:1

While [Jesus] was praying, his face changed in appearance and his clothes became dazzlingly white. Luke 9:28-36

Peter exclaimed on the mountain,
"Master, how good it is for us to be here."
Confident of Christ's presence among us in this assembly,
let us pray for his gifts of healing and transformation:

- For our Church and parish community,
  that we may be faithful to our covenant
  of trust and peace in God:
  let us pray to the Lord.

- For Pope N., Bishop N., Father N.,
  and all who serve the Church as pastors and teachers,
  that they may guide us
  in the way of Christ, the Servant of God:
  let us pray to the Lord.

- For the leaders of governments and nations,
  that they may work unceasingly to re-create our world
  in the peace and justice of God:
  let us pray to the Lord.

- For those experiencing loss or crisis in their lives,
  that, with our compassionate support and kindness,
  they may transform their heartache into joy,
  their despair into hope:
  let us pray to the Lord.

- For those who are preparing
  for baptism and reception into the Church,
  that their hearts may be opened to the Word of God's own Son:
  let us pray to the Lord.

- [For . . .,
  that . . .:
  let us pray to the Lord.]

- For all who have died in Christ's peace
  [especially _____],
  that they may take their places with the citizenry of heaven:
  let us pray to the Lord.

- For the prayers we now make in the silence of our hearts
  [Pause . . .]:
  let us pray to the Lord.

Father, hear the prayers we make before you.
May your Spirit of love and peace
transfigure us and our world
into the image of Jesus, the Risen Christ,
in whose name we offer these prayers.

(God calls to Moses from the burning bush.) Exodus 3:1-8, 13-15

The [experience of the Israelites in the desert] serve as an example.
1 Corinthians 10:1-6, 10-12

(The parable of the unproductive fig tree) Luke 13:1-9

In confidence, let us now offer our prayers to God,
the Lord who is "slow to anger and abounding in kindness":

- That our Church and parish family may pursue,
  with hope and determination,
  the possibilities for forgiveness and reconciliation
  in every relationship and experience:
  let us pray to the Lord.

- That those who serve our Church
  as bishops, pastors, ministers, and teachers
  may speak the Word of God with joyful perseverance:
  let us pray to the Lord.

- That all nations and peoples may work together
  to eradicate persecution, injustice, and hatred from our world:
  let us pray to the Lord.

- That students and young people may,
  like the young Moses,
  respond to the call to become God's messengers
  of compassion and reconciliation:
  let us pray to the Lord.

- [That . . .:
  let us pray to the Lord.]

- That we may respond to God's call
  to alleviate the suffering of the poor,
  to seek justice for the persecuted,
  and to come to the aid of the homeless and hungry:
  let us pray to the Lord.

- That the souls of our deceased relatives and friends
  [especially _____ *],*
  will be welcomed by Christ into the presence of his Father:
  let us pray to the Lord.

- That the God of mercy will hear the prayers we now offer
  in the silence of our hearts
  [Pause . . .]:
  let us pray to the Lord.

Merciful God, hear the prayers of your people,
who struggle, like the fig tree,
to grow in the light of your love.
As you are patient with us,
    may we be patient with one another;
as you forgive us without condition or limits,
    may we forgive one another;
as you hear our cries to you,
    may we hear the cries of one another.
We make these prayers in the name of your Son,
our Lord and Redeemer, Jesus Christ.

The Lord said to Joshua, "Today I have removed the reproach of Egypt from you."
Joshua 5:9, 10-12

In [Christ] we might become the very holiness of God. 2 Corinthians 5:17-21

(The parable of the Prodigal Son) Luke 15:1-3, 11-32

With hearts and voices raised as one,
let us offer our prayers to God
in the name of Jesus, the Lord of reconciliation:

- For our Church and parish community,
  that all may find a place of welcome and hope in our midst:
  let us pray to the Lord.

- For Pope N., Bishop N., Father N.,
  and all who serve the Church,
  that they may be ministers of reconciliation
  and models of forgiveness:
  let us pray to the Lord.

- For the nations and governments of the world,
  that they may be committed to the protection
  and just distribution of the earth's resources:
  let us pray to the Lord.

- For families and households,
  especially those experiencing difficult times,
  that God's Spirit of reconciling love may dwell among them:
  let us pray to the Lord.

- [For . . .,
  that . . .:
  let us pray to the Lord.]

- For the sick, the suffering, and the dying,
  that they may experience the healing presence of Christ
  in our compassion and care:
  let us pray to the Lord.

- For our deceased relatives and friends
  [*especially* _____],
  that they may be re-created in the "holiness of God":
  let us pray to the Lord.

- For the prayers we now offer in the silence of our hearts
  [*Pause . . .*]:
  let us pray to the Lord.

May these prayers, O Lord,
be the beginning of our re-creation
in your love and forgiveness.
With faith in your ever present guidance,
with constant hope in the possibilities of reconciliation,
may we make all things new
in the peace and compassion of Christ Jesus,
in whose name we offer these prayers.

See, I am doing something new!   Isaiah 43:16-21

I have accounted all else rubbish so that Christ may be my wealth.   Philippians 3:8-14

"Let the [one] among you who has no sin be the first to cast a stone at her."
                                                             John 8:1-11

Through Christ, we are constantly called back to God.
With hope, then, let us offer our prayers in Jesus' name:

- That Christ may be the "wealth"
  of our Church and parish community:
  let us pray to the Lord.

- That Pope N., and the bishops, priests,
  and ministers of our Church
  may instruct us in God's ways of peace and reconciliation:
  let us pray to the Lord.

- That the justice and peace of God
  may spring forth in our world
  through cooperation and trust
  among all nations and peoples:
  let us pray to the Lord.

- That we may acknowledge our need for forgiveness
  and seek reconciliation with those who have harmed us:
  let us pray to the Lord.

- That the lives of those entrapped by their addictions
  or enslaved by abuse
  may be "grasped by Christ"
  and made new in his healing peace:
  let us pray to the Lord.

- [For . . .,
  that . . .:
  let us pray to the Lord.]

- That those who have died in the peace of Christ
  [especially _____]
  may come to know the "power flowing from his Resurrection":
  let us pray to the Lord.

- That our gracious God will hear the prayers
  we now offer in the silence of our hearts
  [Pause . . .]:
  let us pray to the Lord.

We lift our hearts to you, O Lord—
you who grasp the lives of the fallen,
who transform our tears into laughter,
who remembers not our past
but constantly makes all things new.
May we be worthy of your limitless forgiveness
and unconditional love
by our forgiveness and love of one another.
In Jesus' name, we pray.

PALM SUNDAY

See Year A.

THE EASTER TRIDUUM

See Year A.

EASTER SUNDAY

See Year A.

Through the hands of the apostles, many signs and wonders occurred among the people.
Acts 5:12-16

*"I am the First and the Last and the One who lives. Once I was dead but now
I live—forever and ever."* Revelation 1:9-11, 12-13, 17-19

[Jesus said] to Thomas: . . . "Do not persist in your unbelief, but believe!"
John 20:19-31

In peace,
let us offer our prayers for the human family:

- For our Church and parish community,
  that our prayer and work together
  may echo the faith proclaimed by Thomas:
  let us pray to the Lord.

- For Pope N., Bishop N., Father N.,
  and for all who lead and serve the Church,
  that they may be ministers of forgiveness
  and prophets of peace:
  let us pray to the Lord.

- For all Christian Churches and communities,
  that Christ may be the cornerstone of their life together:
  let us pray to the Lord.

- For the nations and peoples of the world,
  that the gift of Christ's peace may be theirs:
  let us pray to the Lord.

- [For . . .,
  that . . .:
  let us pray to the Lord.]

- For the sick, the troubled, and the struggling,
  that we may bring healing to their lives
  through our compassion and care:
  let us pray to the Lord.

- For the faithful who have died
  [especially _____],
  that they may live forever in the light of the Risen Christ:
  let us pray to the Lord.

- For the prayers we now make in the silence of our hearts
  [Pause . . .]:
  let us pray to the Lord.

Grant us, O Lord, your peace:
the peace that enables us to constantly discover your joy;
the peace that impels us to seek your justice in all things;
the peace that allows us to suffer for what is right and good;
the peace that invites us to call
   every man, woman, and child "friend."
Hear the prayers we offer for peace—
the peace of Jesus Christ, our Lord and Risen Savior,
who lives and reigns with you for ever and ever.

The apostles . . . left the Sanhedrin full of joy that they had been judged worthy of ill-treatment for the sake of the Name. Acts 5:27-32, 40-41

"Worthy is the Lamb that was slain to receive . . . honor and glory and praise!
Revelation 5:11-14

(Jesus shows himself to the disciples at the Sea of Tiberias.)
"Simon, Son of John, do you love me more than these?" John 21:1-19

Let us join our voices with all of creation
in prayer and praise to our God:

- For our Church and parish community,
  that we may bring the new life of Christ
  into our homes and community
  through forgiveness and reconciliation:
  let us pray to the Lord.

- For Pope N., Bishop N., Father N.,
  and for all who serve the Church,
  that they may proclaim the gospel of the Resurrection
  with courage and perseverance:
  let us pray to the Lord.

- For all the world's nations and peoples,
  that they may work together
  to protect and harvest justly the gifts of the earth:
  let us pray to the Lord.

- [For . . .,
  that . . .:
  let us pray to the Lord.]

- For those who are persecuted for their faith and beliefs,
  that, in their sufferings,
  the justice and peace of God may be exalted:
  let us pray to the Lord.

- For those suffering the pain of illness
  and the hardship of loss or poverty,
  that the riches and strength of God may be theirs:
  let us pray to the Lord.

- For our deceased relatives and friends
  [especially _____ *]*,
  that they may take their places
  at the feast of the Lamb of God:
  let us pray to the Lord.

- For the prayers we now make in the silence of our hearts
  [Pause . . .]:
  let us pray to the Lord.

Gracious God,
hear these prayers of ours for all of humankind.
May we bring the Spirit of Easter into our lives
by recognizing in others the face of the Risen Jesus,
who lives and reigns with you and the Holy Spirit
for ever and ever.

(Paul and Barnabas preach to the Gentiles of Antioch.) Act 13:14, 43-52

"[The Lamb] will lead them to springs of life-giving water, and God will wipe every tear from their eyes." Revelation 7:9, 14-17

"My sheep hear my voice. . . . I give them eternal life, and they shall never perish." John 10:27-30

Let us lift our hearts and voices in prayer to God
in the name of Jesus, the Good Shepherd:

- That our Church and parish community
  may always hear the voice of Christ our Shepherd:
  let us pray to the Lord.

- That the ministries and service
  of our Church's bishops, priests, and teachers
  may be a "light to the nations"
  and a "means of salvation" for all people:
  let us pray to the Lord.

- That the Lamb of God will shepherd
  all nations, races, and peoples
  in the ways of God's justice and peace:
  let us pray to the Lord.

- [That . . .:
  let us pray to the Lord.]

- That the voice of Jesus, the Good Shepherd,
  may transform the hearts of those who promote division,
  hatred, and bigotry in our society:
  let us pray to the Lord.

- That, in our loving support and kindness,
  God will wipe away the tears of the poor,
  the forgotten, and the embittered:
  let us pray to the Lord.

- That the faithful who have died
  [*especially* _____]
  may possess the eternal life won by Christ:
  let us pray to the Lord.

- That God will hear the prayers
  we now make in the silence of our hearts
  [*Pause . . .*]:
  let us pray to the Lord.

As we ask you to hear these prayers, O God,
help us to hear your voice
calling us to compassion and humility,
enabling us to bring the life of the Easter promise
into our homes and communities.
We ask this in the name of Jesus, the Good Shepherd,
who lives and reigns with you for ever and ever.

(The preaching of Paul and Barnabas) "We must undergo many trials if we are to enter into the reign of God." Acts 14:21-27

I, John, saw a new heaven and a new earth. . . . I also saw a new Jerusalem, . . . "God's dwelling among men." Revelation 21:1-5

"This is how all will know you for my disciples: your love for one another." John 13:31-33, 34-35

In Jesus, God has made "all things new."
With joyful confidence, then, let us pray:

- For our Church and parish community,
  that all may know us as disciples
  by our love for one another:
  let us pray to the Lord.

- For those who serve the Church
  as pastors, missioners, and teachers,
  that they may proclaim the good news of the reign of God:
  let us pray to the Lord.

- For the world's nations, cities, and urban areas,
  that they may work together
  to create the "new Jerusalem"—
  God's city of justice and peace:
  let us pray to the Lord.

- For families and households,
  that God may forever dwell in their midst:
  let us pray to the Lord.

- [For . . .,
  that . . .:
  let us pray to the Lord.]

- For those who grieve and mourn,
  for those overcome by loss or broken relationships,
  that God will wipe away the tears from their eyes
  and renew their lives in hope:
  let us pray to the Lord.

- For our deceased relatives and friends
  [especially _____],
  that they may enter into the reign of God:
  let us pray to the Lord.

- For the prayers we now make in the silence of our hearts
  [Pause . . .]:
  let us pray to the Lord.

Hear our Easter prayers, O Lord.
May your Spirit of love make its dwelling among us
so that we may be your people,
your holy city of newness and love.
We offer these prayers in the name of your Son,
our Lord Jesus Christ,
who lives and reigns with you for ever and ever.

" 'It is the decision of the Holy Spirit . . . not to lay on you any burden beyond that which is strictly necessary.' " Acts 15:1-2, 22-29

God gave [the holy city of Jerusalem] it[s] light, and its lamp was the Lamb. Revelation 21:10-14, 22-23

"The Holy Spirit . . . will instruct you in everything. . . . My peace is my gift to you." John 14:23-29

The Risen Jesus is present in the midst of this holy assembly.
With confidence and hope, then,
let us offer our prayers to God in his name:

- That God's word of mercy and compassion
  may be the center of our life together
  as a Church and parish community:
  let us pray to the Lord.

- That those who serve the Church as pastors and ministers
  may dedicate themselves to the cause of the gospel:
  let us pray to the Lord.

- That Christ's farewell gift of peace may be embraced
  by all nations, cities, races, and peoples:
  let us pray to the Lord.

- That the Paraclete, the Holy Spirit,
  may lead us beyond disagreement and division
  to unity and healing:
  let us pray to the Lord.

- [That . . .:
  let us pray to the Lord.]

- That we may hear,
  in the suffering and pain of the poor and persecuted,
  the voice of the Paraclete:
  let us pray to the Lord.

- That those who have died in the peace of Christ
  [especially _____]
  may dwell forever in the holy city of God:
  let us pray to the Lord.

- That our gracious God will hear the prayers
  we now offer in the silence of our hearts
  [Pause . . .]:
  let us pray to the Lord.

Hear our prayers, O Lord,
as we celebrate our Easter rebirth.
Remake our hearts and recast our spirits
to make of us
a fitting dwelling place for you
and your Son, the Risen Christ,
who lives and reigns with you for ever and ever.

ASCENSION OF THE LORD

See Year A.

(The death of Stephen) "Lord, do not hold this sin against them." Acts 7:55-60

"I am the Alpha and the Omega . . . the Beginning and the End . . .
the Morning Star shining bright." Revelation 22:12-14, 16-17, 20

"I pray also for those who will believe in me through [my disciples'] word."
John 17:20-26

Let us offer our prayers to God
in the name of Jesus, the eternal Morning Star:

- For our Church and parish,
  that we may be a community made whole and complete
  in the life and love of God:
  let us pray to the Lord.

- For Pope N., Bishop N., Father N.,
  and for all who serve our Church,
  that they may speak the Word of God
  with conviction and integrity:
  let us pray to the Lord.

- For our President and governor
  and for all the leaders of nations and states,
  that they may build bridges of trust and cooperation
  among all peoples:
  let us pray to the Lord.

- For those to be ordained to the priesthood and diaconate,
  for seminarians, postulants, and novices,
  and for those preparing for lives of service,
  that they may reveal in their ministries
  the depth of God's love for all:
  let us pray to the Lord.

- For the Stephens of our world—
  those who suffer ridicule, persecution and death
  for their witness to the reign of God—
  that they may share in the glory of that reign:
  let us pray to the Lord.

- [For . . .,
  that . . .:
  let us pray to the Lord.]

- For the deceased members of our families and community
  [*especially* _____],
  that they may enter the gates of God's holy city:
  let us pray to the Lord.

- For the prayers we now offer in the silence of our hearts
  [*Pause . . .*]:
  let us pray to the Lord.

Gracious God, hear the prayers of the people
your Son has gathered before you.
May every prayer we utter
and every work we undertake
be to your glory
as we await the fulfillment of the Easter promise in our lives.
We ask these things in the name of your Son, the Risen Jesus,
who lives and reigns with you for ever and ever.

PENTECOST

See Year A.

The Lord begot [the Wisdom of God], the first-born of his ways, the forerunner of his prodigies of long ago. Proverbs 8:22-31

This hope will not leave us disappointed. Romans 5:1-5

"The Spirit of truth . . . will guide you to all truth." John 16:12-15

The goodness of God's creation,
the selfless love of Christ the Redeemer,
the Spirit of God's love in our midst
fill us with wonder.
Confident of God's loving presence among us,
let us pray as one family:

- For the Church, the people of God,
  that the Spirit of truth may guide and inspire us
  to seek and rejoice in the truth:
  let us pray to the Lord.

- For those who serve the Church as pastors and ministers,
  that they may proclaim the great love of God—
  the love revealed to us by Christ Jesus
  and now present among us in the Holy Spirit:
  let us pray to the Lord.

- For the nations and peoples of the world,
  that they may recognize the sacredness of God's creation,
  working together for its just use and protection:
  let us pray to the Lord.

- For parents, teachers, and all who are entrusted
  with the care and education of children,
  that, through their own example of love and selflessness,
  they may help our sons and daughters
  grow in the wisdom and knowledge of God:
  let us pray to the Lord.

- [For . . .,
  that . . .:
  let us pray to the Lord.]

- For the sick, the suffering, the troubled, and the dying,
  that they may once again experience
  the hope which "will not leave us disappointed":
  let us pray to the Lord.

- For those who have died in the peace of Christ
  [especially _____],
  that they may walk forever in the presence of God:
  let us pray to the Lord.

- For the prayers we now offer in the silence of our hearts
  [Pause . . .]:
  let us pray to the Lord.

Gracious God, we call out to you,
not as a mysterious, cosmic riddle,
but as you have made yourself known to us:
    the God of compassion and love,
    the God who redeems us and restores us to life,
    the God who lives in us and through us.
Help us to love others as you love us,
without condition, without limit.
We make these prayers to you,
the Father, Son, and Spirit,
who lives and reigns for ever and ever.

Melchizedek, king of Salem, brought out bread and wine,
and being a high priest of God Most High, he blessed Abram.   Genesis 14:18-20

"This is my body, which is for you. Do this in remembrance of me."
Ｉ   1 Corinthians 11:23-26

Jesus raised his eyes to heaven, pronounced a blessing over [the bread and fishes],
broke them, and gave them to his disciples for distribution to the crowd.   Luke 9:11-17

God invites us to this table
to share the Body and Blood of Jesus in the Eucharist.
Let us raise our hearts and voices in prayer that,
through the Eucharist we are about to celebrate,
we might become eucharist for others:

- That we may be bread for one another—
  a parish community of support and compassion:
  let us pray to the Lord.

- That we may be bread for our world,
  proclaiming with courage and conviction
  the gospel of justice, mercy, and peace:
  let us pray to the Lord.

- That we may be bread for our children,
  teaching them the many wonderful things
  that God has done for us:
  let us pray to the Lord.

- That we may be bread for the poor and hungry,
  willingly sharing with them
  from the bounty we have been given:
  let us pray to the Lord.

- That we may be bread for all in need,
  welcoming all who come to our table
  in search of support, compassion, and understanding:
  let us pray to the Lord.

- [That we may be bread for . . .:
  let us pray to the Lord.]

- That all our deceased relatives and friends
  [especially _____]
  may feast on the Bread of Life forever
  at God's heavenly table:
  let us pray to the Lord.

- That we may be bread for all in need
  through the prayers we now offer
  in the silence of our hearts
  [Pause . . .]:
  let us pray to the Lord.

Gracious Father, Giver and Nurturer of all life,
hear our prayers.
May the bread and wine of the Eucharist
make us bread for one another and for all,
that we might become ministers of your life and love
to our hurting world.
We ask this in the name of Jesus, the Bread of Life.

As a bridegroom rejoices in his bride, so shall your God rejoice in you. Isaiah 62:1-5

There are different gifts but the same Spirit. 1 Corinthians 12:4-11

Jesus performed this first of his signs at Cana in Galilee. John 2:1-12

In confidence and hope,
let us now come before the Lord in prayer:

- For our Church and parish community,
  that we may be a sign to the world
  of God's great love and compassion:
  let us pray to the Lord.

- For those who serve the Church
  as pastors, ministers, and teachers,
  that they may help us discover
  the great things God has done for us:
  let us pray to the Lord.

- For all nations, states, and governments,
  that they may seek justice and equality for all God's people:
  let us pray to the Lord.

- For married couples,
  that Christ the Wedding Guest
  may always be present to them in their life together:
  let us pray to the Lord.

- [For . . .,
  that . . .:
  let us pray to the Lord.]

- For the poor, the homeless, and the forgotten,
  that we may welcome them to our tables:
  let us pray to the Lord.

- For our deceased relatives and friends
  [especially _____],
  that they may take their places
  at the eternal wedding feast of Christ the Bridegroom:
  let us pray to the Lord.

- For the prayers we now make in the silence of our hearts
  [*Pause . . .*]:
  let us pray to the Lord.

Gracious God, open our hearts and minds to your Spirit,
the Spirit of holiness and graciousness
that prompts us to offer these prayers to you—
prayers we ask in the name of your Son, our Lord Jesus Christ.

Ezra read plainly from the book of the law of God, interpreting it so that all could understand what was read. Nehemiah 8:2-4, 5-6, 8-10

You . . . are the body of Christ. 1 Corinthians 12:12-30

"Today this Scripture passage is fulfilled in your hearing." Luke 1:1-4, 4:14-21

Inspired by the Spirit of God present among us,
let us give voice to our prayers for all God's people:

- That, in all of our parish's ministries,
  we may proclaim God's "favor" for all humanity:
  let us pray to the Lord.

- That our Church may be a community of enablement,
  encouraging and supporting all men, women, and children
  to use their gifts and talents
  for the building up of the body of Christ:
  let us pray to the Lord.

- That the nations and peoples of the world
  may embrace God's Spirit of joy, liberty, and peace:
  let us pray to the Lord.

- That those who teach and proclaim the gospel
  may reveal to their students and hearers
  Jesus' vision of compassion and hope:
  let us pray to the Lord.

- [That . . .:
  let us pray to the Lord.]

- That we may reach out
  with patient understanding and support
  to those imprisoned by poverty, abuse, or addiction:
  let us pray to the Lord.

- That all who have died in Christ's peace
  [*especially* _____]
  may realize the promise of the Resurrection:
  let us pray to the Lord.

- That God will hear the prayers we now make
  in the silence of our hearts
  [Pause . . .]:
  let us pray to the Lord.

God of graciousness, hear our prayers.
May your law of justice and mercy
and the gospel of compassion and humility
not shackle us into debating legalisms and narrow interpretations,
but free us to seek and do your will in all things.
In Jesus' name, we pray.

Before you were born I dedicated you, a prophet to the nations I appointed you.

Jeremiah 1:4-5, 17-19

If I have faith . . . but have not love, I am nothing.   1 Corinthians 12:31–13:13

"No prophet gains acceptance in his native place."   Luke 4:21-30

In Christ Jesus, God's promise of salvation
"is fulfilled in [our] hearing."
In confidence, then, let us pray:

- That we may live the gospel of justice and forgiveness
  in our homes, schools, and workplaces:
  let us pray to the Lord.

- That our Church and parish may be a place of welcome
  to all who come to our doors:
  let us pray to the Lord.

- That the nations of the world
  may find lasting peace in their common pursuit
  of justice and liberation for all people:
  let us pray to the Lord.

- That we may hear the voices of the prophets among us,
  calling us to feed the hungry,
  welcome the homeless and the lost,
  and liberate those enslaved
  by poverty, persecution, or addiction:
  let us pray to the Lord.

- [That . . .:
  let us pray to the Lord.]

- That Christ the Healer may restore to health and hope
  the sick, the suffering, and the dying:
  let us pray to the Lord.

- That those who have died
  [especially _____]:
  may live again in the presence of the God of limitless love:
  let us pray to the Lord.

• That God will hear the prayers we now offer
  in the silence of our hearts
  [Pause . . .]:
  we pray to the Lord.

Gracious God,
hear the prayers of the people
formed in the Spirit of your love.
May that love be the fire
that gives warmth and light to our Church;
may that love be the prism through which we see our world;
may that love be the treasure we seek all our days.
We ask these things in the name of Jesus,
your Love incarnate.

I heard the voice of the Lord saying, "Whom shall I send? Who will go for us?"
"Here I am," I said, "send me!" Isaiah 6:1-2, 3-8

By God's favor I am what I am. 1 Corinthians 15:1-11

"Do not be afraid. From now on you will be catching men." Luke 5:1-11

Let us join with the song of the angels and saints
in praise and petition before God:

- That, in our parish's worship and ministries,
  we may proclaim the gospel of the Risen Christ:
  let us pray to the Lord.

- That all who serve the Church
  as pastors, ministers, and teachers
  may faithfully carry on the apostles' work
  of building up the body of Christ:
  let us pray to the Lord.

- That all Churches and faith communities
  may be partners in "catching" souls
  in the net of God's love and forgiveness:
  let us pray to the Lord.

- That the nations and peoples of the world
  may sing together
  a song of peace and thanksgiving to the Creator of all:
  let us pray to the Lord.

- [That . . .:
  let us pray to the Lord.]

- That those who are separated and estranged
  from the love of God
  and the love of family and friends
  may be restored, like Paul,
  to communion with God
  and community with us:
  let us pray to the Lord.

- That all who have died in the peace of Christ
  [especially _____]
  may sing the praises of the Lord
  in the presence of the angels forever:
  let us pray to the Lord.

- That God will hear the prayers we now make
  in the silence of our hearts
  [Pause . . .]:
  let us pray to the Lord.

With hearts filled with gratitude
for all you have done for us, O God,
and with joyful hope in your blessings to come,
we ask you to grant these prayers we offer to you
in the name of your Son, our Lord Jesus Christ.

Blessed is the man who trusts in the Lord, whose hope is the Lord. He is like a tree planted beside the waters that stretches out its roots to the stream. Jeremiah 17:5-8

If Christ was not raised, your faith is worthless. 1 Corinthians 15:12, 16-20

"Blest are you who hunger; you shall be filled. [But] woe to you who are full; you shall go hungry." Luke 6:17, 20-26

To God, the Author of love and Source of hope,
let us offer our prayers:

- For our Church and parish family,
  that we may become a living, nurturing community of faith:
  let us pray to the Lord.

- For the leaders of the world's nations,
  that they may seek justice and equality
  for all peoples:
  let us pray to the Lord.

- For those who serve our Church
  as bishops, priests, deacons, and ministers,
  that they may faithfully and effectively proclaim
  the gospel of the Resurrection:
  let us pray to the Lord.

- [For . . .,
  that . . .:
  let us pray to the Lord.]

- For those who are persecuted and ridiculed for their faith,
  that, through their witness,
  God's mercy and justice may triumph:
  let us pray to the Lord.

- For those who mourn,
  for those who are coping with loss or broken relationships,
  for those who have lost hope,
  that they may find, in our care and support,
  joy, hope, and fulfillment:
  let us pray to the Lord.

- For all who have died
  [*especially* _____],
  that Christ will raise them up
  to the glory of his Resurrection:
  let us pray to the Lord.

- For the prayers we now offer in the silence of our hearts
  [*Pause . . .*]:
  let us pray to the Lord.

Deliver us, O God, from the poverty of selfishness;
enrich us with the treasure of humble giving;
feed us with the bread of your life and love.
Hear these prayers we offer to you
in the name of your Son, our Lord Jesus Christ.

*(David spares Saul.) "Though the Lord delivered you into my grasp,
I would not harm the Lord's anointed."*   1 Samuel 26:2, 7-9, 12-13, 22-23

[Christ,] the last Adam, has become a life-giving spirit.   1 Corinthians 15:45-49

"Love your enemies, do good to those who hate you."   Luke 6:27-38

To God, the Author of love, let us pray:

- That, in our life together as a Church and parish,
  we may seek the love of God in all things:
  let us pray to the Lord.

- That those who serve our Church
  as bishops, priests, preachers, and ministers
  may be dedicated to the work
  of reconciliation and forgiveness:
  let us pray to the Lord.

- That the nations and peoples of the world
  may tear down the walls which divide them
  and build between them
  bridges of respect, understanding, and peace:
  let us pray to the Lord.

- That institutions of government, education, and finance
  may be guided in the conduct of all human affairs
  by God's Spirit of justice and mercy:
  let us pray to the Lord.

- [That . . .:
  let us pray to the Lord.]

- That we may recognize the person of Jesus
  in those who "beg" from us,
  who sin against us,
  and who cry out to us in desperation:
  let us pray to the Lord.

- That the faithful who have died
  [especially _____]
  may rise with Christ to newness of life:
  let us pray to the Lord.

- That God will hear the prayers
  we now make in the silence of our hearts
  [Pause . . .]:
  let us pray to the Lord.

Lord God, make us worthy disciples of your Son:
may we give without counting the cost;
may we pardon without setting conditions;
may we seek peace without demanding control or power.
In our faithfulness to your Son's teachings,
may we make these prayers we ask a reality.
In Jesus' name, we pray.

The fruit of a tree shows the care it has had.   Sirach 27:4-7

Thanks be to God who has given us the victory through our Lord Jesus Christ.
                                        1 Corinthians 15:54-58

"A good tree does not produce decayed fruit any more than a decayed tree produces good fruit."
                                        Luke 6:39-45

Let us now pray together
that our hope in God's great love
will reap a harvest of blessings for all the human family:

- For our Church and parish,
  that we may sow and reap a harvest
  of compassion, justice, and mercy:
  let us pray to the Lord.

- For Pope N., Bishop N., Father N.,
  and the bishops, priests, and deacons of our Church,
  that they may proclaim the love of God
  with humility, understanding, and integrity:
  let us pray to the Lord.

- For our country and for all nations and peoples,
  that together we may build a world
  dedicated to peace and justice
  and free of hatred, poverty, and oppression:
  let us pray to the Lord.

- For parents and teachers,
  that, in their love for their children,
  they may help them discover the wisdom and love of God:
  let us pray to the Lord.

- [For . . .,
  that . . .:
  let us pray to the Lord.]

- For the sick, the suffering, and the dying,
  that the love of Christ may be their hope:
  let us pray to the Lord.

- For the faithful who have died
  [especially _____],
  that they may share in Christ's victory over sin and death:
  let us pray to the Lord.

- For the prayers we now make in the silence of our hearts
  [Pause . . .]:
  let us pray to the Lord.

We lift our prayers to you, O Lord of hope,
confident that you will continue to bless us.
Nurture us in your love,
that we may sow and reap a harvest of joy.
Grant these prayers we make
in the name of your Son, Jesus Christ.

(Solomon's prayer) "To the foreigner [who honors you] . . . listen from your heavenly dwelling."   1 Kings 8:41-43

If I were trying to win man's approval, I would surely not be serving Christ.
                                                    Galatians 1:1-2, 6-10

(Jesus saves the life of the centurion's servant.)   Luke 7:1-10

Let us now offer our prayers to our heavenly Father,
who hears us when we call:

- For our Church and parish community,
  that the Risen Christ may find
  a worthy dwelling place in our midst:
  let us pray to the Lord.

- For those called to proclaim the gospel,
  that they may persevere in the ministry
  entrusted to them by Christ:
  let us pray to the Lord.

- For all nations, states, and cities,
  that they may seek to build bridges of peace and justice
  among the peoples of the world:
  let us pray to the Lord.

- For those who govern the affairs of humankind,
  that they may lead with compassion, humility, and justice:
  let us pray to the Lord.

- For those who do not know God
  or who no longer practice their faith,
  that they may discover, in us,
  the mercy and healing love of God:
  let us pray to the Lord.

- [For . . .,
  that . . .:
  let us pray to the Lord.]

- For the sick, the suffering, and the dying,
  that the favor of God may be their hope and strength:
  let us pray to the Lord.

- For all who have died
  [especially _____],
  that the light of Christ's peace may shine upon them:
  let us pray to the Lord.

- For the prayers we now make in the silence of our hearts
  [Pause . . .]:
  let us pray to the Lord.

Father, we come together as a people of faith,
confident of your love and compassion.
Hear the prayers we offer—
prayers which your Spirit
inspires us to ask of you
in the name of Jesus Christ, our Lord.

(Elijah's prayer for the widow's son) "O Lord, my God, let the life breath return to the body of this child." 1 Kings 17:17-24

The gospel I proclaim to you is no mere human invention. Galatians 1:11-19

(At Naim, Jesus raises up the son of the widow.) Luke 7:11-17

Great is the compassion of God for all people.
Let us, therefore, confidently make known to the Lord
the needs of our human family:

- For our Church and parish community,
  that all may come to know, in us,
  the compassion and forgiveness of God:
  let us pray to the Lord.

- For Pope N., Bishop N., Father N.,
  and for all bishops, priests, deacons, and ministers,
  that the word of the Lord may come truly from their mouths:
  let us pray to the Lord.

- For the nations and peoples of the world,
  that God's Spirit of understanding and peace
  may dwell in all lands:
  let us pray to the Lord.

- For those who minister to the sick and dying,
  especially their family and friends,
  that they may find joyful fulfillment
  in the compassion and care they give:
  let us pray to the Lord.

- [For . . .,
  that . . .:
  let us pray to the Lord.]

- For those grieving the loss of loved ones,
  especially those who mourn the deaths of sons and daughters,
  that God's hope may sustain them
  as they continue their life's journeys:
  let us pray to the Lord.

- For our deceased relatives and friends
  [especially _____],
  that they may be raised up by Christ
  to the life of his Resurrection:
  let us pray to the Lord.

- For the prayers we now offer in the silence of our hearts
  [Pause . . .]:
  let us pray to the Lord.

Compassionate Father, hear these prayers for ourselves
and for all your holy people.
Transform our hopelessness into faith,
change our mourning into dancing,
and lift our spirits from death to life.
In Jesus' name, we pray.

Nathan answered David: "The Lord on his part has forgiven your sin:
you shall not die."   2 Samuel 12:7-10, 13

I have been crucified with Christ, and the life I live now is not my own.
                                                        Galatians 2:16, 19-21

"She has washed my feet with her tears and wiped them with her hair. . . .
That is why her many sins are forgiven—because of her great love."   Luke 7:36–8:3

Humbled by the great love and compassion of our God,
let us, with joyful hope, offer our prayers in Jesus' name:

- That our Church and parish community
  may be a place of acceptance and welcome
  to all who come to our doors:
  let us pray to the Lord.

- That those who serve our Church
  as pastors, preachers, and teachers
  may proclaim the love and forgiveness of God:
  let us pray to the Lord.

- That all nations and peoples
  may dispel ancient hatreds and divisions
  and look forward, with hope, to reconciliation and peace:
  let us pray to the Lord.

- That we may always seek to forgive and be reunited
  with those who hurt and harm us,
  just as God always forgives us
  and calls us to return:
  let us pray to the Lord.

- [That . . .:
  let us pray to the Lord.]

- That society's outcasts—
  those who are rejected and scorned—
  may discover, in us, the joy of acceptance
  and the reality of God's love:
  let us pray to the Lord.

- That the faithful who have died
  [especially _____]
  may rise to the new life of the Risen Christ:
  let us pray to the Lord.

- That God will grant the prayers
  we now make in the silence of our hearts
  [Pause . . .]:
  let us pray to the Lord.

Father of compassion and forgiveness,
hear the prayers we offer for ourselves
and for all the members of our human family.
May your Spirit inspire us
to forgive others joyfully
and to seek their forgiveness humbly.
We make these prayers to you in Jesus' name.

They shall look upon him whom they have thrust through, and they shall mourn for him as one mourns for an only son. Zechariah 12:10-11

All are one in Christ Jesus. Galatians 3:26-29

"Whoever wishes to be my follower must deny his very self, take up his cross each day, and follow in my steps." Luke 9:18-24

Let us now lift up our hearts and voices in prayer to the Lord:

- That, through our ministries of prayer and charity,
  our Church and parish may proclaim that Jesus is the Messiah:
  let us pray to the Lord.

- That God will bless Pope N., Bishop N.,
  and all our bishops
  with the courage, faithfulness, and perseverance
  of Peter and the apostles:
  let us pray to the Lord.

- That President N., Governor N.,
  and all who govern the affairs of state
  will seek ways to tear down the walls
  which divide peoples and nations:
  let us pray to the Lord.

- That those who suffer for the sake of justice,
  who are victimized by the greed of others,
  and who are persecuted for their convictions
  may one day know the victory of the cross:
  let us pray to the Lord.

- [That . . .:
  let us pray to the Lord.]

- That the God of compassion and kindness
  will uphold the sick, the suffering, the recovering, and the dying:
  let us pray to the Lord.

- That the faithful who have died
  [especially _____]
  may find, in the presence of God, light, happiness, and peace:
  let us pray to the Lord.

- That God will grant the prayers
  we now make in the silence of our hearts
  [Pause . . .]:
  let us pray to the Lord.

Gracious God, hear the prayers we lift up to you.
Give us the courage and the generosity
to crucify our self-centeredness
and take up our crosses to follow Christ,
so that we may bring his life and liberation to our world.
We offer these prayers in the name of Jesus,
the Messiah and Redeemer.

The Lord said to Elijah: "You shall anoint Elisha . . . as prophet to succeed you."
1 Kings 19:16, 19-21

Out of love, place yourselves at one another's service. Galatians 5:1, 13-18

"Whoever puts his hand to the plow but keeps looking back is unfit for the reign of God."
Luke 9:51-62

Let us now place our hearts and voices
at one another's service
to pray for the needs
of all our brothers and sisters in Christ:

- That we may embrace the life of selflessness and commitment
  that Jesus demands of those who would be his disciples:
  let us pray to the Lord.

- That those who serve the Church
  as pastors, teachers, and counselors
  may be ministers of forgiveness and reconciliation:
  let us pray to the Lord.

- That families and households
  may always realize and celebrate
  the love of Christ living in their midst:
  let us pray to the Lord.

- That God will bless the work
  of farmers and food producers,
  so that their harvest may be a blessing,
  especially for those who are hungry and starving:
  let us pray to the Lord.

- [That . . .:
  let us pray to the Lord.]

- That those who are enslaved
  by any form of addiction or abuse
  may be freed from the yoke of their suffering
  through our love, understanding, and support:
  let us pray to the Lord.

- That God will raise up to the new life of the Son
  the souls of our deceased relatives and friends
  [especially _____]:
  let us pray to the Lord.

- That God will bless those for whom we now pray
  in the silence of our hearts
  [Pause . . .]:
  let us pray to the Lord.

Hear the prayers we make to you, O Lord,
for all of our brothers and sisters.
Give us the courage, vision, and commitment
to be prophets of your great love for humankind
and authentic disciples of the Risen Christ,
in whose name we make these prayers.

As a mother comforts her son, so will I comfort you. Isaiah 66:10-14

May I never boast of anything but the cross of our Lord Jesus Christ!

Galatians 6:14-18

"The harvest is rich but the workers are few." Luke 10:1-12, 17-20

Let us join our hearts and voices in prayer
for all who journey with us to the kingdom of God:

- For our Church and parish community,
  that every work and prayer of ours
  may proclaim the compassion and peace of God:
  let us pray to the Lord.

- For all bishops, priests, and deacons,
  and for the members of religious orders and communities,
  that their lifestyles of simplicity, charity, and peace
  may give joyful witness to the reign of God:
  let us pray to the Lord.

- For the nations and peoples of the world,
  that God may bless them with peace and prosperity forever:
  let us pray to the Lord.

- For college students and young adults,
  that the Spirit of God will open their hearts
  to take on the work of the harvest:
  let us pray to the Lord.

- [For . . .,
  that . . .:
  let us pray to the Lord.]

- For those who suffer
  from illness, persecution, loss, or addiction,
  that they may find comfort in the healing love of God:
  let us pray to the Lord.

- For all who have died in the peace of Christ
  [especially _____],
  that they may rise with him to newness of life:
  let us pray to the Lord.

- For the prayers we now make in the silence of our hearts
  [Pause . . .]:
  let us pray to the Lord.

Hear our prayers, O Lord,
and be with us on our journey.
May your peace guide our steps
and your hope light our way
as we journey through this life
to the joy of your kingdom,
where you live and reign for ever and ever.

Moses said to the people: . . . "This command which I enjoin on you today is . . .
already in your mouths and in your hearts." Deuteronomy 30:10-14

Christ Jesus is the image of the invisible God, the first-born of all creatures.
Colossians 1:15-20

(The parable of the Good Samaritan) Luke 10:25-37

To the Lord of love and Father of compassion
let us lift up our hearts in prayer:

- That our Church and parish community
  may be a place of welcome
  and a community of support to all our neighbors:
  let us pray to the Lord.

- That all nations, governments, and institutions
  may be committed to making the justice and peace of God
  a reality for all the world's peoples:
  let us pray to the Lord.

- That pastors, preachers, teachers, and religious educators
  may instruct their students
  in the ways of God's love and compassion:
  let us pray to the Lord.

- [That . . .:
  let us pray to the Lord.]

- That those who care for the sick, the recovering, and the dying
  may see, in their patients, the person of Jesus:
  let us pray to the Lord.

- That the victims of violence and abuse
  may be restored to health
  and wholeness of spirit and dignity:
  let us pray to the Lord.

- That those who have died
  [especially _____]
  may experience the peace of the Risen Christ,
  "the first-born of the dead":
  let us pray to the Lord.

- That God will bless those for whom we now pray
  in the silence of our hearts
  [Pause . . .]:
  let us pray to the Lord.

Compassionate God, Father of all humanity,
hear the prayers we offer.
Give us eyes of faith to see all men and women
as our brothers and sisters,
and hearts of love to welcome them as your children.
We make this prayer through Christ our Lord.

The Lord appeared to Abraham by the terebinth of Mamre. Genesis 18:1-10

I became a minister of this church through the commission God gave me to preach among you his word in its fullness. Colossians 1:24-28

"Mary has chosen the better portion and she shall not be deprived of it."
Luke 10:38-42

Let us now come before the Lord in prayer:

- For our Church and parish community,
  that we may seek "the better portion"—
  the will of God in all things:
  let us pray to the Lord.

- For Pope N., Bishop N., Father N.,
  and for the bishops, priests, and ministers of our Church,
  that they may be faithful to their "commission"
  to preach the word of God "in its fullness":
  let us pray to the Lord.

- For the nations and peoples of the world,
  that they may welcome and accept
  all men and women as brothers and sisters:
  let us pray to the Lord.

- For those who serve as cooks, housekeepers, and cleaners,
  for those who provide care and hospitality to travelers,
  that God will bless them for the quality and dignity
  they bring to the lives of others:
  let us pray to the Lord.

- [For . . .,
  that . . .:
  let us pray to the Lord.]

- For those who are persecuted for their principles,
  that their suffering may inspire us
  to seek the justice and mercy of God in all things:
  let us pray to the Lord.

- For those who have died in the peace of Christ
  [*especially* _____],
  that they may be welcomed by the saints and angels
  into the house of God:
  let us pray to the Lord.

- For the prayers we now offer in the silence of our hearts
  [*Pause . . .*]:
  let us pray to the Lord.

Kind and loving Father, hear our prayers.
May we serve you by serving one another
joyfully and sincerely,
compassionately and completely,
just as your Son, Jesus, served and loved us.
We make these prayers in Jesus' name.

"For the sake of those ten [innocent], I will not destroy Sodom."   Genesis 18:20-32

God canceled the bond that stood against us, . . . snatching it up and nailing it to the cross.   Colossians 2:12-14

"Ask, and you shall receive; seek and you shall find."   Luke 11:1-13

Jesus promises that our heavenly Father hears the prayers
of those who come before God in faith.
And so, let us confidently lift up our hearts in prayer:

- That, in our work and worship together,
  our Church and parish may reflect our faith
  in Christ's resurrection:
  let us pray to the Lord.

- That those who serve our Church
  as pastors, teachers, and counselors
  may be ministers of God's reconciling and healing love:
  let us pray to the Lord.

- That those nations, cities, and peoples
  plagued by war, oppression, and destruction
  may be rebuilt in the peace and justice of God:
  let us pray to the Lord.

- [That . . .:
  let us pray to the Lord.]

- That men and women of good will
  may speak, like Abraham,
  on behalf of the innocent victims
  of poverty, oppression, greed, and abuse:
  let us pray to the Lord.

- That the sick, the suffering, and the dying
  may find hope and healing in company with Christ the Redeemer:
  let us pray to the Lord.

- That the Father will raise to the new life of the Risen Jesus
  the souls of all who have died
  [especially _____]:
  let us pray to the Lord.

- That God will hear the prayers
  we now offer in the silence of our hearts
  [Pause . . .]:
  let us pray to the Lord.

Loving Father, we know you hear our prayers.
May the spirit in which we ask these things
inspire us and enable us
to make these prayers a reality.
In Jesus' name, we pray.

Vanity of vanity! All things are vanity.	Ecclesiastes 1:2; 2:21-23
Be intent on things above rather than on things of earth.	Colossians 3:1-5, 9-11
(The parable of the rich man's grain bins)	Luke 12:13-21

Let us offer our prayers to God,
the Giver of life and Source of all that is good:

- That the love of Christ may be the object
  of every prayer and work of our Church and parish community:
  let us pray to the Lord.

- That the laws and policies of governments and nations
  may honor and uphold the sacred dignity of every person:
  let us pray to the Lord.

- That equality and justice may guide the affairs
  of businesses, corporations, and financial institutions:
  let us pray to the Lord.

- That families, households, and communities
  may grow rich in love, compassion, and forgiveness:
  let us pray to the Lord.

- [That . . .:
  let us pray to the Lord.]

- That we may respond to the plight
  of the poor, the homeless, and the destitute
  with unlimited and unconditional generosity:
  let us pray to the Lord.

- That the souls of the faithful departed
  [especially _____]
  may be raised up "in company with Christ":
  let us pray to the Lord.

- That God will hear the prayers
  we now offer in the silence of our hearts
  [Pause . . .]:
  let us pray to the Lord.

Gracious God,
may your Spirit of wisdom and justice
dwell within us always,
guiding us and inspiring us
to work joyfully and unceasingly
to make these prayers a reality.
We ask these things
in the name of your Son, our Lord Jesus Christ.

Your people awaited the salvation of the just. Wisdom 18:6-9

Faith is confident assurance concerning what we hope for, and conviction about things we do not see. Hebrews 11:1-2, 8-19

"Be like men awaiting their master's return from a wedding." Luke 12:32-48

The author of the letter to the Hebrews writes:
"Faith is confident assurance concerning what we hope for,
and conviction about things we do not see."
With confident faith, then, let us pray:

- For our Church and parish community,
  that we may share with the world
  the treasure of our faith in God's providence:
  let us pray to the Lord.

- For the leaders of nations,
  that they may make of this earth
  a homeland of peace and justice
  for all races and peoples:
  let us pray to the Lord.

- For managers, bankers, and economists,
  that they may conduct their business ethically and justly,
  with concern for the needs and aspirations
  of all men and women:
  let us pray to the Lord.

- [For . . .,
  that . . .:
  let us pray to the Lord.]

- For missionaries
  and for those who have given their lives
  in service to the poor,
  that their priceless witness to the gospel
  will be richly rewarded:
  let us pray to the Lord.

- For the sick, the suffering, and the dying,
  that Christ will be with them
  in their most painful and desperate moments:
  let us pray to the Lord.

- For the faithful who have died
  [especially _____],
  that they dwell forever in the house of God:
  let us pray to the Lord.

- For the prayers we now offer in the silence of our hearts
  [Pause . . .]:
  let us pray to the Lord.

From age to age, O God, you show your love for us.
From generation to generation you call us back to you.
Hear the prayers we offer you this day.
Give us your grace
to recognize your presence in the things we see,
and to trust in your providence in the things we do not see.
We make our prayer through Christ our Lord.

"Jeremiah ought to be put to death; he demoralizes the soldiers . . . and all the people, by speaking such things." Jeremiah 38:4-6, 8-10

Let us keep our eyes fixed on Jesus, who inspires and perfects our faith.
Hebrews 12:1-4

"I have come to light a fire on the earth." Luke 12:49-53

Let us put aside those things which divide us
and come together in prayer for the needs of all people:

- For our Church and parish community,
  that in our worship and work together,
  we may keep our vision always fixed on the Risen Christ:
  let us pray to the Lord.

- For Pope N., Bishop N., Father N.,
  for all bishops, priests, and deacons,
  and for all ministers of our Church,
  that they may persevere in their proclamation
  of God's justice and peace:
  let us pray to the Lord.

- For the leaders of nations, states, and cities,
  that they may seek justice and equality
  for the people and communities they serve:
  let us pray to the Lord.

- For families and households in crisis,
  that they may rediscover love and selflessness
  in the example of Christ Jesus:
  let us pray to the Lord.

- [For . . .,
  that . . .:
  let us pray to the Lord.]

- For the poor, the abused, and the abandoned,
  that we may work to overturn and transform
  the systems and obstacles that impoverish them:
  let us pray to the Lord.

- For the souls of those who have died
  [especially _____ *],*
  that the Risen Christ may deliver them
  to the "throne of God":
  let us pray to the Lord.

- For the prayers we now offer in the silence of our hearts
  [Pause . . .]:
  let us pray to the Lord.

Gracious Father, hear these prayers of ours.
May your Holy Spirit extinguish division and discord among us
and ignite a blaze of compassion, justice, and hope within us.
We ask these things in the name of your Son,
our Light and Hope, Jesus Christ.

I come to gather nations of every language.   Isaiah 66:18-21

Make straight the paths you walk on.   Hebrews 12:5-7, 11-13

(The parable of the narrow door) "People will come from the east and the west,
from the north and the south, and take their place at the feast in the kingdom of God."
Luke 13:22-30

We come to the Lord's table as a community of faith.
In that same spirit,
let us offer our prayers for the needs of all people:

- That our parish community may be a place
  of support and affirmation
  as we struggle through the "narrow door"
  to the reign of God:
  let us pray to the Lord.

- That our Church may realize and celebrate
  its catholic nature,
  welcoming and honoring the peoples
  of every nation and culture
  who come to this table:
  let us pray to the Lord.

- That all nations may journey together in peace
  to the holy mountain of God:
  let us pray to the Lord.

- That the new academic year
  [beginning in the next few weeks]
  may be a time of discovery and fulfillment
  for both students and teachers:
  let us pray to the Lord.

- That, in their selfless love and care for their families,
  parents and guardians may teach their children
  the limitless and unconditional love of God:
  let us pray to the Lord.

- [That . . .:
  let us pray to the Lord.]

- That our relatives and friends who have died
  [especially _____]
  may find light and peace in the presence of God forever:
  let us pray to the Lord.

- That God will grant the prayers we now make
  in the silence of our hearts
  [Pause . . .]:
  let us pray to the Lord.

Father of all nations, hear the prayers we offer.
May the spirit of community which brings us together
    at this Eucharistic table
bring us and all people together one day
    at your table in your heavenly kingdom,
where Jesus is Lord for ever and ever.

Humble yourself the more, the greater you are.   Sirach 3:17-18, 20, 28-29

You have drawn near to . . . the city of the living God, the heavenly Jerusalem.
                                                                   Hebrews 12:18-19, 22-24

*"Those who exalt themselves shall be humbled, and those who humble themselves
shall be exalted."*   Luke 14:1, 7-14

Humbled by the realization of God's great love for us,
let us pray:

- That, in the ministries of our Church and parish community,
  we may seek to extend the love of God
  without limitations, conditions, or expectations:
  let us pray to the Lord.

- That our bishops, priests, deacons, and ministers
  may imitate the humility of Christ, the Servant of God:
  let us pray to the Lord.

- That the nations and peoples of the world
  may cooperate in peace and trust
  to establish "the city of the living God":
  let us pray to the Lord.

- [That . . .:
  let us pray to the Lord.]

- That the poor, the abused, the lost, and the forgotten
  may find places of honor and welcome at our tables and altars:
  let us pray to the Lord.

- That the sick, the suffering, the recovering, and the dying
  may be reassured of the great love of God
  in the compassionate care and humble service
  we joyfully extend to them:
  let us pray to the Lord.

- That the souls of our deceased relatives and friends
  [*especially* _____]
  may be welcomed by God to the banquet of heaven:
  let us pray to the Lord.

- That God will grant the prayers we now make
  in the silence of our hearts
  [Pause . . .]:
  let us pray to the Lord.

Hear the prayers we make to you, O gracious Father.
In all of creation,
in your gift of life itself,
you have shown your great love for your human family.
May we give you thanks for your many blessings
by living lives that are worthy of such love.
We make these prayers to you
in the name of Jesus, our Lord and Savior.

What man knows God's counsel, or who can conceive what the Lord intends?
Wisdom 9:13-18

You might possess him forever, no longer as a slave but as more than a slave,
a beloved brother. Philemon 9-10, 12-17

"Anyone who does not take up his cross and follow me cannot be my disciple."
Luke 14:25-33

When we come to this table,
we put aside discord and division
to offer, in peace and unity,
the one bread and the one cup.
In that spirit then, let us pray:

- That, as a Church and parish community,
  we may joyfully take up Jesus' cross
  of selflessness and compassion:
  let us pray to the Lord.

- That the ministry of Pope N.,
  and the bishops, pastors, and teachers of our Church
  may help humankind discover
  the grace of God "within our grasp":
  let us pray to the Lord.

- That the Risen Christ may be a source
  of unity, liberation, and justice
  for all families, nations, and peoples:
  let us pray to the Lord.

- That parents and teachers
  may help their children and students
  discover and grow in the wisdom of God:
  let us pray to the Lord.

- [That . . .:
  let us pray to the Lord.]

- That those who are enslaved by drugs and alcohol
  may find, among us, the courage and support
  to free themselves from their addictions:
  let us pray to the Lord.

- That our deceased relatives and friends
  [especially _____]
  may be welcomed by Christ into his Father's kingdom:
  let us pray to the Lord.

- That God will grant the prayers we now make
  in the silence of our hearts
  [Pause . . .]:
  let us pray to the Lord.

Father of mercy, Lord of compassion,
hear our prayers.
Inspired by your Spirit dwelling within us,
may we honor every person
with the love, dignity, and acceptance
due them as your sons and daughters.
We ask this through Christ our Lord.

Moses implored the Lord, his God, saying, "Why, O Lord, should your wrath blaze up against your own people?" Exodus 32:7-11, 13-14

The grace of our Lord has been granted me in overflowing measure. 1 Timothy 1:12-17

"There will . . . be more joy in heaven over one repentant sinner than over ninety-nine righteous people." Luke 15:1-32

Let us come before the Lord of mercy
in prayer for all God's people:

- That our parish community
  may be a place of reconciliation and forgiveness
  for the lost, the abandoned, and the alienated:
  let us pray to the Lord.

- That Pope N., and our bishops, priests, and deacons
  may be ministers of God's mercy and forgiveness:
  let us pray to the Lord.

- That those nations and countries
  in political and economic turmoil
  may work together to establish peace and justice
  for all their citizens:
  let us pray to the Lord.

- That we may not be obsessed
  with consumerism and materialism
  but seek the values of the gospel in all things:
  let us pray to the Lord.

- [That . . .:
  let us pray to the Lord.]

- That those whose journeys through life
  are marked by illness, suffering, grief, and despair
  may find, in us, support and consolation:
  let us pray to the Lord.

- That God will raise up
  to the new life of the Son's resurrection
  the souls of our deceased relatives and friends
  [especially _____]:
  let us pray to the Lord.

- That God will grant the prayers we now make
  in the silence of our hearts
  [Pause . . .]:
  let us pray to the Lord.

Loving Father, we come to you in prayer for all people.
In imitation of your Son
may we search out the lost,
welcome the poor to our table,
and accompany the suffering and grieving on their journey,
    bearing, with them, their pain and anguish.
We ask this in the name of him who welcomed sinners,
our Lord and Redeemer, Jesus Christ.

311

Never will I forget [what those who trample upon the needy] have done! Amos 8:4-7

I urge that petitions, prayers, intercessions, and thanksgivings be offered for all men, especially for . . . those in authority. 1 Timothy 2:1-8

(The parable of the unscrupulous manager) Luke 16:1-13

Christ is present in our midst.
Let us join our hearts and minds
to become one community of prayer,
asking God's blessing upon all people:

- For our Church and parish,
  that a spirit of prayer may transform us
  into a community of love and compassion:
  let us pray to the Lord.

- For our President and governor,
  and for all in government service,
  that they may work ceaselessly
  to protect the rights and dignity of all men, women, and children:
  let us pray to the Lord.

- For business men and women,
  for corporations and all financial institutions,
  that their quest for profits
  may not blind them to their responsibility
  to uphold the common good:
  let us pray to the Lord.

- For those who use, develop, and protect the environment,
  that God's gift of the earth
  may be used in the service of the rich and poor alike
  for generations to come:
  let us pray to the Lord.

- [For . . .,
  that . . .:
  that let us pray to the Lord.]

- For the sick and the suffering,
  for the poor and the needy,
  that they may know the goodness of God
  in our compassion and care:
  let us pray to the Lord.

- For the faithful who have died
  [especially _____],
  that they may possess the life won for them by Christ:
  let us pray to the Lord.

- For the prayers we now make in the silence of our hearts
  [Pause . . .]:
  let us pray to the Lord.

Father, may the spirit of our prayers
live on in every moment of life you give us,
so that we may seek first
your justice and peace in all things.
In Jesus' name, we pray.

The complacent in Zion . . . shall be the first to go into exile, and their wanton revelry shall be done away with. Amos 6:1, 4-7

Take firm hold on the everlasting life to which you were called. 1 Timothy 6:11-16

(The parable of Lazarus and the rich man) Luke 16:19-31

For all of our brothers and sisters,
let us offer our prayers to God, the Father of us all:

- For our Church and parish community,
  that we may respond with courage and conviction
  to Christ's call to discipleship:
  let us pray to the Lord.

- For our Holy Father, our bishop, and our pastor,
  and for all who serve our Church,
  that they may be effective and tireless teachers of faith
  and prophets of justice:
  let us pray to the Lord.

- For our President, governor,
  and all legislators, judges, and government officials,
  that they may be dedicated to the principles
  of equality, liberty, and justice for all:
  let us pray to the Lord.

- For businesses, banks, and corporations,
  that they may be builders of God's holy city
  of peace, justice, and liberty:
  let us pray to the Lord.

- For the poor and unwanted Lazaruses at our own gates—
  that they may find places of welcome and honor at our tables:
  let us pray to the Lord.

- [For . . .,
  that . . .:
  let us pray to the Lord.]

- For all who have died in the peace of Christ
  [especially _____],
  that they may be "carried by angels"
  to the heavenly banquet of God:
  let us pray to the Lord.

- For the prayers we now make in the silence of our hearts
  [Pause . . .]:
  let us pray to the Lord.

Open our eyes, O Lord,
to see the poor, the grieving, and the destitute
at our own doors;
open our hearts
to welcome them to our tables
and share with them
the many good things you have given us.
We make our prayer to you, Father,
in the name of Jesus Christ, your Son, our Risen Lord.

The vision still has its time, presses on to fulfillment, and will not disappoint.
Habakkuk 1:2-3, 2:2-4

Guard the rich deposit of faith with the help of the Holy Spirit. 2 Timothy 1:6-8, 13-14

(The parables of the mustard seed and the dutiful servants) Luke 17:5-10

Confident that God hears the prayers we make in faith,
let us pray in Jesus' name:

- For our Church and parish community,
  that we may seek to be servants
  of the poor, the lost, and the defenseless:
  let us pray to the Lord.

- For Pope N., Bishop N., Father N.,
  and for all bishops, priests, and deacons,
  that they may teach and share with all God's people
  the "rich deposit of faith":
  let us pray to the Lord.

- For the nations and peoples of the world,
  that the peace and justice of God
  may overcome violence, oppression, and hatred:
  let us pray to the Lord.

- For parents, teachers, counselors, and educators,
  that they may share with their children and students
  God's vision that "will not disappoint":
  let us pray to the Lord.

- [For . . .,
  that . . .:
  let us pray to the Lord.]

- For those in pain,
  for those who have given up hope,
  especially the addicted, the homeless, and the imprisoned,
  that they may possess the faith of the "mustard seed"
  enabling them to rebuild their lives:
  let us pray to the Lord.

- For the deceased members of our families and community,
  [especially _____ *],*
  that they may live forever in the light of God's love:
  let us pray to the Lord.

- For the prayers we now make in the silence of our hearts
  [Pause . . .]:
  let us pray to the Lord.

Gracious Father,
you have given us life and hope
for no other reason than your great love for us.
May this realization inspire us
in every moment of our lives
to be your faithful servants
by being servants to one another.
Hear these prayers we offer to you
in the name of your Son, our Lord Jesus Christ.

Naaman went down and plunged into the Jordan seven times at the word of Elisha.
2 Kings 5:14-17

If we have died with [Christ], we shall also live with him. 2 Timothy 2:8-13

One of [the lepers, a Samaritan], realizing that he had been cured, came back praising God in a loud voice. Luke 17:11-19

Let us now raise our voices in prayer to the God of mercy:

- That every program and project of our parish
  may manifest a spirit of thankfulness
  for God's many blessings:
  let us pray to the Lord.

- That those who serve our Church
  as bishops, priests, deacons, and ministers
  may never cease to proclaim
  the forgiveness and compassion of God:
  let us pray to the Lord.

- That the world's nations and peoples
  may find cause for unity and peace
  in sharing with one another
  the gifts of God's good earth:
  let us pray to the Lord.

- That scientists, medical researchers, and technicians
  may be blessed with knowledge and perseverance
  as they seek to alleviate human suffering and pain:
  let us pray to the Lord.

- [That . . .:
  let us pray to the Lord.]

- That the sick and dying may experience,
  in our care and compassion,
  the healing presence of Christ:
  let us pray to the Lord.

- That those who have died in the peace of Christ
  [especially _____ *]*
  may rise with him to newness of life:
  let us pray to the Lord.

- That God will hear the prayers we now make
  in the silence of our hearts
  [Pause . . .]:
  let us pray to the Lord.

Father of compassion, God of mercy,
you are never far away from us,
you never cease to hear our cries.
We beg your blessing upon the good that we do,
and your healing of the ills that afflict us.
In Jesus' name, we pray.

As long as Moses kept his hands raised up, Israel had the better of the fight.

Exodus 17:8-13

I charge you to preach the word, to stay with this task whether convenient or inconvenient . . . never losing patience. 2 Timothy 3:14–4:2

(The parable of the corrupt judge and the persistent widow) Luke 18:1-8

Confident that God hears the prayers we make in faith,
let us raise our hearts and voices in prayer:

- For our parish community,
  that a spirit of servanthood may guide us
  in our worship and work together:
  let us pray to the Lord.

- For preachers and religious educators,
  that they may teach God's holy word
  with wisdom and perseverance:
  let us pray to the Lord.

- For judges, attorneys, and court officers,
  that a respect for God's justice and mercy
  will inspire their deliberations and decisions:
  let us pray to the Lord.

- For the members of the military services
  and those charged with the defense of our nation,
  that they may carry out their duties
  with a conscientious commitment to justice:
  let us pray to the Lord.

- [For . . .,
  that . . .:
  let us pray to the Lord.]

- For the victims of any form of abuse
  and for their families,
  that their dignity may be restored
  and their goodness affirmed
  through our loving care and support:
  let us pray to the Lord.

- For the deceased members of our families and community
  [*especially* _____],
  that they may walk forever in the light of the Risen Christ:
  let us pray to the Lord.

- For the prayers we now make in the silence of our hearts
  [*Pause . . .*]:
  let us pray to the Lord.

Father, we call to you, knowing that you hear our prayers.
May our voicing of them as one family
inspire us to work as one family
to make these prayers a reality.
In Jesus' name, we pray.

The prayer of the lowly pierces the clouds.   Sirach 35:12-14, 16-18

I have finished the race, I have kept the faith. From now on a merited crown awaits me.
2 Timothy 4:6-8, 16-18

(The parable of the Pharisee and the tax collector)   Luke 18:9-14

Humbled by the depth of God's love for us,
let us pray:

- That our Church and parish may constantly offer to God
  the prayer of service to the poor and forgotten:
  let us pray to the Lord.

- That Pope N., Bishop N., Father N.,
  and all who serve the Church
  may imitate the humility of Christ
  in their proclamation of his gospel:
  let us pray to the Lord.

- That nations and governments may work together
  to tear down the walls of anger, hatred, and intolerance
  that divide peoples and communities:
  let us pray to the Lord.

- That those who administer public programs and monies
  may always realize their sacred responsibility
  to the public trust:
  let us pray to the Lord.

- [That . . .:
  let us pray to the Lord.]

- That our compassionate care and unconditional support
  of the poor, the needy, the abused, and the addicted
  may make us worthy of their prayers before God:
  let us pray to the Lord.

- That the faithful who have died
  [*especially* _____]
  may dwell forever in the kingdom of God:
  let us pray to the Lord.

- That God will hear the prayers we now make
  in the silence of our hearts
  [Pause . . .]:
  let us pray to the Lord.

Father of compassion,
Lord of all that is good,
you love us without limit,
you accept us as your own without condition.
In a spirit of joyful humility,
may we, too, learn to love one another
without limit or condition.
We offer these prayers
in the name of Jesus Christ our Lord.

You love all things that are and loathe nothing that you have made.

Wisdom 11:22–12:1

We pray for you always that our God may make you worthy of his call.

2 Thessalonians 1:11–2:2

"Zacchaeus, hurry down. I mean to stay at your house today." Luke 19:1-10

Our God is a God of mercy and forgiveness—
the Creator who loves "all things that are."
In confidence, then, let us call upon God in prayer:

- That our Church and parish community
  may be a place of welcome to all people,
  especially the poor, the hurting, and the forgotten:
  let us pray to the Lord.

- That we may recognize and accept in others,
  especially those who are ignored and shunned by society,
  the gifts they have to offer to the human family:
  let us pray to the Lord.

- That we may honor the Lord of creation
  through our just stewardship of God's gifts of the earth:
  let us pray to the Lord.

- That we may approach death
  not in terror and fear
  but with confident faith and hope
  in God's promise of the Resurrection:
  let us pray to the Lord.

- [That . . .:
  let us pray to the Lord.]

- That the great compassion of God
  will restore to health and give hope to the sick,
  the suffering, the recovering, and the dying:
  let us pray to the Lord.

- That the Risen Christ will welcome into his Father's kingdom
  the souls of our deceased relatives and friends
  [especially _____]:
  let us pray to the Lord.

- That God will hear the prayers
  we now offer in the silence of our hearts
  [Pause . . .]:
  let us pray to the Lord.

Father, we see your hand in everything that is good.
Give us eyes of faith to see your imperishable Spirit
in every member of the human family.
May we welcome them as guests among us
as you will welcome us one day
into your eternal dwelling place.
We offer these prayers to you in Jesus' name.

"It is my choice to die at the hands of men with the God-given hope of being restored to life by him."   2 Maccabees 7:1-2, 9-14

May God who . . . gave us eternal consolation and hope, console your hearts and strengthen them for every good work and word.   2 Thessalonians 2:16–3:5

"Those judged worthy of a place in the age to come . . . are no longer liable to death."
                                                                    Luke 20:27-38

Let us now confidently raise our hearts and voices in prayer
to our heavenly Father, the living God:

- For our Church and parish community,
  that we may respond to Christ's call to discipleship
  through the giving of our time and talents
  to our many parish ministries:
  let us pray to the Lord.

- For missionaries and catechists
  and all who teach the word of God,
  that they may enrich the lives of their hearers
  by revealing the presence of God to them:
  let us pray to the Lord.

- For the members of religious orders and communities,
  that their lives of poverty, chastity, and obedience
  may give joyful witness to this world
  of the life of the world to come:
  let us pray to the Lord.

- [For . . .,
  that . . .:
  let us pray to the Lord.]

- For those who fight for the rights of the oppressed,
  that the Spirit of God will strengthen them
  with perseverance and hope:
  let us pray to the Lord.

- For the sick and recovering,
  for those who mourn and despair,
  that the God of mercy will console their hearts
  and lift their spirits with hope:
  let us pray to the Lord.

- For those who have died in the peace of Christ
  [*especially* _____],
  that the God of the living may restore them to life:
  let us pray to the Lord.

- For the prayers we now make in the silence of our hearts
  [*Pause . . .*]:
  let us pray to the Lord.

Father, hear these prayers—
prayers which you inspire us to make.
May the good that we do in this time and place
make us sons and daughters
of the Resurrection of your Son, our Lord Jesus Christ,
who lives and reigns with you for ever and ever.

For you who fear my name, there will arise the sun of justice. Malachi 3:19-20

You know how you ought to imitate us. 2 Thessalonians 3:7-12

"I will give you words and a wisdom which none of your adversaries can take exception to or contradict." Luke 21:5-19

Let us now offer our prayers to God our Father
in the name of Christ, the "Sun of Justice":

- For our Church and parish community,
  that our ministries of prayer and service to all
  may be signs of hope to our world:
  let us pray to the Lord.

- For those who serve our Church
  as bishops, priests, pastors, and teachers,
  that they may speak to all the world
  Christ's word of reconciliation and peace:
  let us pray to the Lord.

- For the nations and peoples of the world,
  that the peace of God may reign
  in all human relationships and endeavors:
  let us pray to the Lord.

- For families and friends divided,
  that they may put aside anger, jealousy, and hatred
  for the sake of the love of God:
  let us pray to the Lord.

- For those who are persecuted for their faith
  or ridiculed for their beliefs,
  that their witness to the truth
  may reign over the ignorance of their persecutors:
  let us pray to the Lord.

- [For . . .,
  that . . .:
  let us pray to the Lord.]

- For our deceased relatives and friends
  [especially _____],
  that the light of Christ's peace may shine upon them forever:
  let us pray to the Lord.

- For the prayers we now offer in the silence of our hearts
  [Pause . . .]:
  let us pray to the Lord.

Gracious God,
open our hearts and spirits
to see your light in the darkest of nights,
to feel your presence in the most hopeless of hours.
Hear the prayers we offer to you
in the name of your Son, Jesus Christ,
the Sun of Justice.

The Lord said to David, "You shall shepherd my people Israel and shall be commander of Israel." 2 Samuel 5:1-3

Christ is the image of the invisible God, the first-born of all creatures. Colossians 1:12-20

"I assure you: this day you will be with me in paradise." Luke 23:35-43

In joyful hope, let us offer our prayers to God in the name of Jesus, who reconciles everything "on earth and in the heavens":

- That our Church and parish community
  may be a faithful witness
  to the love and mercy of our heavenly Father:
  let us pray to the Lord.

- That Pope N., Bishop N., Father N.,
  and all who serve the Church
  may be teachers of God's peace
  and ministers of reconciliation among all people:
  let us pray to the Lord.

- That President N., Governor N.,
  and all legislators, judges, and civil authorities
  may serve our nation, state, and city
  with wisdom and compassion:
  let us pray to the Lord.

- [That . . .:
  let us pray to the Lord.]

- That we may proclaim the great mystery of God's love
  through our compassion and charity
  to the poor, the homeless, and the abandoned:
  let us pray to the Lord.

- That Jesus, our Redeemer, may restore to health and hope
  the sick, the suffering, the recovering, and the dying:
  let us pray to the Lord.

- That our deceased relatives and friends
  [*especially* _____]
  may be welcomed by the victorious Christ into paradise:
  let us pray to the Lord.

- That the God of mercy and compassion
  will hear the prayers we now offer
  in the silence of our hearts
  [*Pause . . .*]:
  let us pray to the Lord.

We praise you, O God,
you who are Lord of creation
and Father of all nations.
Hear the prayers we offer in joyful hope
until the coming of our Messiah and King,
our Lord Jesus Christ,
who lives and reigns with you and the Holy Spirit
as one God,
for ever and ever.

SOLEMNITIES AND HOLY DAYS

February 2: PRESENTATION OF THE LORD

There will come to the temple the Lord whom you seek.　　　　Malachi 3:1-4

[Jesus] had to become like his brothers . . . that he might be a merciful and faithful high priest before God on their behalf.　　　　Hebrews 2:14-18

(Simeon's prophecy concerning the child) "A revealing light to the Gentiles, the glory of your people Israel."　　　　Luke 2:22-40

In Christ Jesus, we have seen the very depth of God's love.
In confidence, then,
let us offer our prayers to God in Jesus' name:

- For our Church and parish community,
  that the light of Christ may shine forth from within us:
  let us pray to the Lord.

- For our bishops, priests, and deacons,
  and for all who serve the Church,
  that they may be faithful messengers and prophets
  of God's presence among us:
  let us pray to the Lord.

- For the world's nations and peoples,
  that they may be instruments of God's justice and peace:
  let us pray to the Lord.

- For parents and guardians,
  that the love of God may be with them and their children
  in both times of joy and times of sorrow:
  let us pray to the Lord.

- For all children,
  that they may learn and grow in wisdom and grace
  within the joy of a loving family:
  let us pray to the Lord.

- [For . . .,
  that . . .:
  let us pray to the Lord.]

- For the poor and suffering,
  that, through our support and assistance to them,
  they may rediscover the joy of God's great love:
  let us pray to the Lord.

- For all the faithful who have died
  [especially _____],
  that Simeon and Anna and all the saints
  may welcome them into the new Jerusalem:
  let us pray to the Lord.

- For the prayers we now make in the silence of our hearts
  [Pause . . .]:
  let us pray to the Lord.

O Lord, come and shatter the darkness of our world
with the light of your love.
May these prayers we offer
and our work to bring them to fulfillment
bring the light and peace of Christ into our own time and place.
We make these prayers to you in the name of Christ our Light.

June 24: NATIVITY OF JOHN THE BAPTIST

VIGIL MASS:

Before you were born I dedicated you, a prophet to the nations I appointed you.

Jeremiah 1:4-10

This is the salvation which the prophets carefully searched out and examined.

1 Peter 1:8-12

"God himself will go before [John], in the spirit and power of Elijah, . . . to prepare for the Lord a people well-disposed."
Luke 1:5-17

MASS OF THE DAY:

I will make you a light to the nations, that my salvation may reach to the ends of the earth.
Isaiah 49:1-6

John heralded the coming of Jesus by proclaiming a baptism of repentance to all the people of Israel.
Acts 13:22-26

[Zechariah] signaled for a writing tablet and wrote the words, "His name is John."
Luke 1:57-66, 80

Like John the Baptizer,
we have been called
to speak God's Word to our world.
Let us pray now that we may be worthy of that call:

- That our Church and parish community may be a light
  of God's love and compassion for the human family:
  let us pray to the Lord.

- That Pope N., Bishop N., Father N.,
  and all who serve the Church
  may be heralds of Jesus, God's Word made flesh:
  let us pray to the Lord.

- That the "coastlands" and "distant peoples" of the world
  may one day be gathered in justice and peace before God:
  let us pray to the Lord.

- That parents and teachers
  may share with their children and students
  the wisdom and knowledge of God:
  let us pray to the Lord.

- [That . . .:
  let us pray to the Lord.]

- That the poor and sick,
  the troubled and oppressed,
  and those who suffer with them
  may be restored to health and wholeness
  through the love of Christ:
  let us pray to the Lord.

- That our deceased relatives and friends
  [especially _____ *]*
  may be reborn in the light and peace of the Risen Savior:
  let us pray to the Lord.

- That we may be ministers of hope and reconciliation
  in the prayers we now offer in the silence of our hearts
  [Pause . . .]:
  let us pray to the Lord.

Gracious God, hear our prayers.
Transform our lives and our world
    from barrenness to harvest,
    from sickness to wholeness,
    from division to completeness,
    from death to life.
We offer these prayers to you
in the name of your Son, our Lord Jesus Christ.

June 29: PETER AND PAUL, Apostles

VIGIL MASS:

Peter said [to the man crippled from birth], "In the name of Jesus Christ the Nazorean, walk!" Acts 3:1-10

The gospel I proclaimed to you is no mere human invention. Galatians 1:11-20

[Peter said to Jesus]: "Lord, you know everything. You know well that I love you." John 21:15-19

MASS OF THE DAY:

Peter . . . said, "Now I know for certain that the Lord has sent his angel to rescue me from Herod's clutches and from all that the Jews hoped for." Acts 12:1-11

I have fought the good fight, I have finished the race, I have kept the faith. 2 Timothy 4:6-8, 17-18

"You are the Messiah," Simon Peter answered, "the Son of the living God!" Matthew 16:13-19

Through Peter and Paul and the apostles
we have heard the good news of the gospel.
With hope, then, let us lift our voices in prayer
to God, the Father of our Lord Jesus Christ:

- For our Church and parish,
  that every prayer and work of ours
  may proclaim that Jesus is the Messiah:
  let us pray to the Lord.

- For Pope N. and the bishops of our Church,
  that they may faithfully continue the teaching mission
  begun by Peter and the apostles,
  that "all the nations might hear the gospel":
  let us pray to the Lord.

- For those who serve the Church as pastors and teachers,
  that they may be ministers of reconciliation
  and agents of God's forgiveness:
  let us pray to the Lord.

- For those who have dedicated themselves
  to the service of the sick, the poor, and the lost,
  that God may be their strength and joy:
  let us pray to the Lord.

- [For . . .,
  that . . .:
  let us pray to the Lord.]

- For those who, like Paul,
  are persecuted for their faith
  or oppressed for their beliefs,
  that their witness to the truth
  will one day be exalted:
  let us pray to the Lord.

- For those who have died in the peace of Christ
  [especially _____],
  that Peter, Paul, and all the saints
  may welcome them into the kingdom of God:
  let us pray to the Lord.

- For the prayers we now offer in the silence of our hearts
  [Pause . . .]:
  let us pray to the Lord.

Hear the prayers we raise to you, O God,
for all your holy people.
Grant us the constant faith of Peter,
that we may proclaim your presence among us always;
reassure us with the unwavering hope of Paul,
that we may persevere in joy in this life
as we await the life of the world to come.
We ask these things in the name of your Son,
Jesus Christ, the Messiah and Holy One.

August 6: TRANSFIGURATION OF THE LORD

I saw One like a son of man coming, on the clouds of heaven.　　Daniel 7:9-10, 13-14

We were in his company on the holy mountain.　　2 Peter 1:16-19

(Jesus is transfigured before Peter, James, and John.)　　YEAR A: Matthew 17:1-9
YEAR B: Mark 9:2-10
YEAR C: Luke 9:28-36

We echo Peter's exclamation on the mountain:
"Lord [Rabbi] [Master], how good it is for us to be here."
Confident of Christ's presence among us in this assembly,
let us pray for his gifts of healing and re-creation:

- That our Church and parish community
  may light lamps in dark places,
  bringing the love of God into our world:
  let us pray to the Lord.

- For Pope N., Bishop N., Father N.,
  and all who serve the Church as pastors and teachers,
  that they may guide us
  in the way of Christ, the Servant of God:
  let us pray to the Lord.

- For the leaders of nations and governments,
  that they may work ceaselessly
  to remove the threat of nuclear war,
  transforming the fear and tension between enemies
  into trust and respect among neighbors:
  let us pray to the Lord.

- [For . . .,
  that . . .:
  let us pray to the Lord.]

- For those experiencing loss or crisis in their lives,
  that, with our compassionate support and kindness,
  they may transform their heartache into joy,
  their despair into hope:
  let us pray to the Lord.

- For the sick, the suffering, and the dying,
  that Christ, the Morning Star,
  may restore them to health and wholeness:
  let us pray to the Lord.

- For all who have died in Christ's peace
  [especially _____],
  that they may walk forever in the light and peace of God:
  let us pray to the Lord.

- For the prayers we now make in the silence of our hearts
  [Pause . . .]:
  let us pray to the Lord.

Father, hear the prayers we make before you.
May your Spirit of love and peace
transfigure us and our world
in the image of Jesus, the Risen Christ,
in whose name we offer these prayers.

August 15: ASSUMPTION OF MARY

VIGIL MASS:

They set [the ark of God] within the tent which David had pitched for it.
1 Chronicles 15:3-4, 15, 16; 16:1-2

Then will the saying of Scripture be fulfilled: "Death is swallowed up in victory."
1 Corinthians 15:54-57

"Blest are they who hear the word of God and keep it."   Luke 11:27-28

MASS OF THE DAY:

[The woman] gave birth to a son . . . who is destined to shepherd all the nations.
Revelation 11:19; 12:1-6, 10

Christ has been raised from the dead, the first fruits of those who have fallen asleep.
1 Corinthians 15:20-26

(Elizabeth's greeting to Mary): "Blessed are you among women and blessed is the fruit of your womb."   Luke 1:39-56

With confident faith in God,
the Lord who has done great things for us,
let us pray:

- That every ministry and work of our Church and parish
  may proclaim the greatness of God's mercy:
  let us pray to the Lord.

- That our bishops, priests, and ministers,
  and all who serve the Church
  may proclaim the presence of God among us:
  let us pray to the Lord.

- That all nations and peoples
  may seek to raise up the dignity of every person
  made in the image and likeness of God:
  let us pray to the Lord.

- That parents and guardians may see in Mary
  a model of loving patience and selfless devotion:
  let us pray to the Lord.

- [That . . .:
  let us pray to the Lord.]

- That our generous sharing of this year's harvest
  with the poor and hungry
  may be our song of thanks to God our Savior:
  let us pray to the Lord.

- That those who have died in the peace of Christ
  [especially _____]
  may share in Mary's hymn of endless praise:
  let us pray to the Lord.

- That the Lord of mercy will hear the prayers
  we now offer in the silence of our hearts
  [Pause . . .]:
  let us pray to the Lord.

Father, hear the prayers we offer
as we celebrate Mary's Easter,
her sharing in the life of her Risen Son.
May her prayer, the gift of a mother's love,
    be our joy through all ages;
may her faith, the response of a humble heart,
    inspire us to live lives worthy of your promise.
We ask this in the name of our Lord and Savior, Jesus Christ.

September 14: TRIUMPH OF THE CROSS

The Lord said to Moses: "Make a saraph and mount it on a pole, and if anyone who has been bitten looks at it, he will recover."   Numbers 21:4-9

[Christ] humbled himself, obediently accepting even death, death on a cross!
                                                             Philippians 2:6-11

"God so loved the world that he gave his only Son, that whoever believes in him . . . may have eternal life."   John 3:13-17

Jesus' words to Nicodemus fill us with hope:
"God so loved the world that he gave his only Son. . . ."
With joyful confidence, then, let us pray in Jesus' name:

- That our Church and parish community may proclaim,
  in our work and worship together,
  the victory of the cross:
  let us pray to the Lord.

- That Pope N., Bishop N., Father N.,
  and all who serve the Church
  may proclaim the joy and hope of God's salvation:
  let us pray to the Lord.

- That the nations and peoples of the world
  may travel together on this earth
  to God's promised land of justice and peace:
  let us pray to the Lord.

- [That . . .:
  let us pray to the Lord.]

- That we may imitate the attitude
  of the humble and obedient Jesus
  by emptying ourselves
  for the sake of the poor, the fallen, and the helpless:
  let us pray to the Lord.

- That the crucified Christ may lift up
  the sick, the suffering, the recovering, and the dying
  to health and hope:
  let us pray to the Lord.

- That the faithful who have died
  [especially _____]
  may share in the life of the Resurrection
  won for them by Christ on the cross:
  let us pray to the Lord.

- That God will hear the prayers
  we now offer in the silence of our hearts
  [Pause . . .]:
  let us pray to the Lord.

Father of endless love and compassion,
hear the prayers of your family gathered here before you.
May we imitate your Son
by taking up our crosses with joyful obedience,
    seeking your justice in all things;
may we embrace his example of loving humility,
    loving and praising you
    in the compassion and care we extend to one another.
We ask these things in the name of your Son,
Jesus Christ, our Lord and Redeemer.

November 1: ALL SAINTS

"These are the ones who have . . . washed their robes and made them white in the blood of the Lamb." Revelation 7:2-4, 9-14

We are God's children. 1 John 3:1-3

"How blest are the poor in spirit: the reign of God is theirs." Matthew 5:1-12

In the name of Christ Jesus, the hope of saints and sinners,
let us offer our prayers to the Father:

- For our Church and parish family,
  that we may become a people of the Beatitudes—
  seeking God's presence and joy in all things:
  let us pray to the Lord.

- For Pope N., Bishop N., Father N.,
  and for all who serve the Church,
  that their ministry among us may build bridges
  from this life to the eternal life of God:
  let us pray to the Lord.

- For the nations and peoples of the world,
  that they may work together
  to establish God's holy city of peace:
  let us pray to the Lord.

- For families and households,
  especially for children,
  that the saints may inspire them
  to seek the love of Christ in all things:
  let us pray to the Lord.

- [For . . .,
  that . . .:
  let us pray to the Lord.]

- For those who work for equality and justice,
  for those who are persecuted and ridiculed for their beliefs,
  for those who give their lives in humble service to others,
  that their prophetic witness may make the New Jerusalem
  a reality in our world:
  let us pray to the Lord.

346

- For all who have died in the peace of Christ
  [especially _____],
  that the company of the saints may welcome them
  into the kingdom of heaven:
  let us pray to the Lord.

- For the prayers we now make in the silence of our hearts
  [Pause . . .]:
  let us pray to the Lord.

Father, make us children of your light.
May the lives of the saints give us hope
that one day we might be among the blessed of your kingdom.
Give us the courage and resolve
to be saints for our world,
that one day this feast of All Saints
may be *our* feast day as well.
Hear the prayers we make to you in the name of your Son,
our Risen Lord, Jesus Christ.

November 2: ALL SOULS

Readings from the Masses for the Dead (Lectionary, nos. 789–93).

To God, the Father of mercy and the Lord of compassion,
let us pray:

- For our Church and parish family,
  that we may be a community of hope
  in the promise of Jesus' resurrection:
  let us pray to the Lord.

- For the bishops, priests, deacons, and ministers
  who serve our Church,
  that their ministries among us
  may proclaim the good news of Easter's empty tomb:
  let us pray to the Lord.

- For the nations and peoples of the world,
  that God will destroy the hate that divides them
  and bring them together in the ways of justice and peace:
  let us pray to the Lord.

- [For . . .,
  that . . .:
  let us pray to the Lord.]

- For those who mourn the deaths of family and friends,
  that, in our loving support,
  they may find the strength to continue
  their own lives' journeys:
  let us pray to the Lord.

- For the sick, the recovering, and the dying,
  that the compassion of Jesus may be present to them
  in our prayers and care for them:
  let us pray to the Lord.

- For all who have died in the peace of Christ
  [*especially* _____],
  that they may find, in the presence of God,
  light, happiness, and peace:
  let us pray to the Lord.

- For the prayers we now make in the silence of our hearts
  [*Pause . . .*]:
  let us pray to the Lord.

Hear our prayers, O Lord,
and be with us on our journey.
May your peace guide our steps
and hope light our way
as we journey through this life
to the joy of the life of the world to come.
We make our prayers in the name of your Son,
our Risen Lord and Redeemer, Jesus Christ.

November 9: DEDICATION OF ST. JOHN LATERAN

(Jacob's vision of a stairway reaching to the heavens): "Truly the Lord is in this spot . . . !"　　　　　　　　　　　　　　　　　　Genesis 28:11-18

The temple of God is holy, and you are that temple.　　　1 Corinthians 3:9-13, 16-17

Jesus calls to Zacchaeus: "Today salvation has come to this house."　　　Luke 19:1-10

Christ, the "foundation" of this house,
is present in our holy assembly.
With joyful hope, then, let us pray for our human family:

- For our Church and parish community,
  that reconciliation and forgiveness may be
  the foundation of our life together:
  let us pray to the Lord.

- For Pope N.,
  and for our bishops, priests, ministers, and teachers,
  that they may lead all of humankind
  to the threshold of the house of God:
  let us pray to the Lord.

- For the nations and peoples of the world,
  that they may work together unceasingly
  to build the holy city of God's justice and peace:
  let us pray to the Lord.

- For artists and sculptors,
  for weavers and embroiderers,
  for writers, poets, and musicians,
  and for all artisans and crafters,
  that we may behold and celebrate in their work
  the wonder and beauty of God:
  let us pray to the Lord.

- [For . . .,
  that . . .:
  let us pray to the Lord.]

- For the poor, the lost, the addicted, and the abused,
  that the compassionate Jesus may seek them out
  and restore them to health and hope:
  let us pray to the Lord.

- For our deceased relatives and friends
  [especially _____ *]*,
  that they may live forever
  in the eternal dwelling place of God:
  let us pray to the Lord.

- For the prayers we now make in the silence of our hearts
  [Pause . . .]:
  let us pray to the Lord.

Come and make your dwelling place among us, O Lord.
Make of this house a place of healing,
    a place of consolation,
    a place of hope for all who come to its doors;
make of us a temple of your holiness,
    a temple of your forgiveness,
    a temple of your infinite love and compassion.
We offer these prayers to you in the name of your Son,
the Risen Lord, Jesus Christ.

December 8: IMMACULATE CONCEPTION

"I will put enmity between you and the woman, and between your offspring and hers."
Genesis 3:9-15, 20

We were predestined [by God] to praise his glory by being the first to hope in Christ.
Ephesians 1:3-6, 11-12

*(The angel Gabriel is sent to Mary.) "You shall conceive and bear a son. . . .
He will be called Son of the Most High."*
Luke 1:26-38

With the simple faith and heartfelt joy of Mary,
let us offer our prayers to God, the Most High:

- That our parish's ministries of prayer and charity
  may be our joyful acceptance of God's great love for us:
  let us pray to the Lord.

- That the God of mercy and compassion
  may find a worthy dwelling place in our Church:
  let us pray to the Lord.

- That the nations and peoples of the world
  may seek to raise up the dignity of every person
  made in the image and likeness of God:
  let us pray to the Lord.

- That all parents may see in Mary
  a model of loving patience and selfless devotion:
  let us pray to the Lord.

- [That . . .:
  let us pray to the Lord.]

- That Mary's faithful humility may inspire us
  to become generous and compassionate servants
  to the poor, the forgotten, and the desperate:
  let us pray to the Lord.

- That those who have died in God's peace
  [especially _____]
  may share in the eternal reign of Jesus the Christ:
  let us pray to the Lord.

- That our compassionate God will hear the prayers
  we now offer in the silence of our hearts
  [Pause . . .]:
  let us pray to the Lord.

In loving trust and faith, O God,
your daughter Mary accepted your will for her
to bring into the world your Son, the Messiah.
May the prayers we offer to you today
and our work to bring them to fulfillment
bring the light and peace of the Messiah
into our own time and place.
We ask this in the name of your Son,
our Lord and Savior, Jesus the Christ.

OBSERVANCES IN THE UNITED STATES

July 4: INDEPENDENCE DAY

Rejoicing in God's great providence,
let us now offer our prayers
for the needs of our nation
and for all the nations and peoples of the world:

- For the Church in the United States,
  that we may be, for our country,
  faithful prophets of God's justice
  and witnesses to God's great love for all men, women, and children:
  let us pray to the Lord.

- For our nation's leaders, judges, and legislators,
  that God's wisdom may inspire and guide them
  in the conduct of national affairs
  and international diplomacy:
  let us pray to the Lord.

- For all our nation's citizenry,
  that we may give thanks
  for God's many blessings to our nation
  by our commitment to the principles
  of justice, liberty, and equality for all:
  let us pray to the Lord.

- For all nations and peoples of the world,
  that God's Spirit of peace may govern all human affairs:
  let us pray to the Lord.

- [For . . .,
  that . . .:
  let us pray to the Lord.]

- For those in our land who are not free,
  who are enslaved by illness, poverty, and addiction,
  that, with our compassionate help and support,
  they may re-create their lives in hope and purpose:
  let us pray to the Lord.

- For all who have died,
  especially those who have given their lives
  in our nation's service,
  that God may gather them into the kingdom of heaven:
  let us pray to the Lord.

- For the prayers we now make in the silence of our hearts
  [Pause . . .]:
  we pray to the Lord.

God of mercy, Lord of peace,
hear the prayers we make to you on this day
when we celebrate our nation's birth.
Make us truly a nation united.
May our land be a harbor of peace and unity
for all people, races, faiths, and cultures
until the coming of your kingdom,
where you live and reign for ever and ever.

Fourth Thursday of November: THANKSGIVING DAY

Let us join our hearts and raise our voices in prayer
to the Lord of the harvest:

- For our Church and parish community,
  that we may be a people dedicated to thankfulness:
  let us pray to the Lord.

- For Pope N., Bishop N., Father N.,
  and all who serve our Church,
  that they may proclaim the love and mercy of God
  to all people:
  let us pray to the Lord.

- For our country and the people of this land,
  that we may be faithful and generous stewards
  of God's creation:
  let us pray to the Lord.

- For the nations and peoples of the world,
  that the justice and mercy of God
  may be the cornerstone of lasting peace:
  let us pray to the Lord.

- For families in crisis
  and for those in despair,
  that they may always know
  the love and support of family and friends:
  let us pray to the Lord.

- For the grieving and the troubled,
  for the abused and the addicted,
  that we may reach out to them
  in compassion and understanding:
  let us pray to the Lord.

- For the sick and the suffering,
  that they may experience the presence of the healing Christ:
  let us pray to the Lord.

- For those who have died,
  that they may find in the presence of God
  light, happiness, and peace:
  let us pray to the Lord.

- For the prayers we now make in the silence of our hearts
  [Pause . . .]:
  let us pray to the Lord.

Father of love, Lord of creation,
we give you thanks for your many blessings to us:
for the gifts of the earth
    which sustain and nurture our lives,
for the gifts of your Spirit
    which make our lives complete and whole in your love.
May we give you thanks for your many gifts
by sharing those gifts with one another;
may we be worthy of your great love for us
by working constantly to make these prayers
for peace and compassion a reality.
We offer these prayers to you, O Father,
in the name of your Son,
our Lord and Savior, Jesus Christ.

RITUAL MASSES

BAPTISM of Children

Let us now offer our prayers
to our Father in heaven,
for the needs of all God's children on earth:

- That these children may grow in wisdom and grace
  within the joy of a loving family:
  let us pray to the Lord.

- That the love of our heavenly Father
  may inspire these fathers, mothers, and godparents
  to fulfill their holy vocation of parenthood
  with love and joy:
  let us pray to the Lord.

- That our Church and parish community
  may accompany these children
  on their journeys to the kingdom of God:
  let us pray to the Lord.

- That all nations and peoples may recognize one another
  as sons and daughters of God:
  let us pray to the Lord.

- That the love of Christ may dwell
  within the homes and hearts
  of all families and households:
  let us pray to the Lord.

- That the sick, the suffering, and the recovering
  may find hope and healing in the compassion of Christ:
  let us pray to the Lord.

- That all our deceased relatives and friends
  [especially _____]
  may rise to the new life of the Risen Christ:
  let us pray to the Lord.

- That God will hear the prayers we now offer
  in the silence of our hearts
  [Pause . . .]:
  let us pray to the Lord.

Heavenly Father,
in the mystery of your great love,
you created us and claimed us as your own;
in Jesus, your Love incarnate,
you created us anew in the promise of his Resurrection.
Hear our prayers for these newly baptized.
May they grow in wisdom and love before you.
May we share with them the gift of faith you have given us
until that day when the promise of the Resurrection
is fulfilled in our lives.
Hear these prayers we offer
in the name of your Son, our Lord Jesus Christ.

BAPTISM of Adults

To God, Giver of all good things,
let us pray:

- For these newly baptized,
  that they may be re-created
  in the new life of the Risen Christ:
  let us pray to the Lord.

- For the families and friends of these newly baptized,
  for their sponsors,
  and for those who prepared them for baptism,
  that they may be a source of encouragement and understanding
  in their journeys to God:
  let us pray to the Lord.

- For our Church and parish,
  that we may be a welcoming and supportive family
  to these new members of our faith community:
  let us pray to the Lord.

- For the nations and peoples of the world,
  that, in Christ, all men and women
  may recognize one another as brothers and sisters:
  let us pray to the Lord.

- For all who serve the poor, the homeless, and the dying,
  that God will bless their work with joy:
  let us pray to the Lord.

- For the sick and the dying,
  for the suffering and the imprisoned,
  for the addicted and the abused,
  that they may be freed from their infirmities
  and re-created in the life of the Risen Christ:
  let us pray to the Lord.

- For our departed brothers and sisters
  [*especially* _____],
  that they may rise to the new life of the victorious Christ:
  let us pray to the Lord.

- For the prayers we now offer in the silence of our hearts
  [Pause . . .]:
    let us pray to the Lord.

Gracious God,
in the waters of baptism
you make us new again in the life of your Risen Son.
Transform us into a community of his disciples,
that the life and love of his Resurrection
may be a constant and lasting reality in our lives.
We ask this through Christ, our Risen Lord.

CONFIRMATION

Just as we are one in faith, hope, and love,
let us come before the Lord as one in prayer:

(NOTE: The following petitions should be adapted if read by a member of the confirmation class.)

- For the members of this confirmation class,
  that, by their [our] word and example,
  they [we] may support and encourage others
  to follow Jesus Christ:
  let us pray to the Lord.

- For their [our] parents, godparents, and sponsors,
  that God will bless them abundantly
  for the faith they have shared with them [us]:
  let us pray to the Lord.

- For our Church and parish community,
  that the Holy Spirit may dwell within
  the life of prayer and charity we share together:
  let us pray to the Lord.

- For Pope N., Bishop N., Father N.,
  for all bishops, priests, religious brothers and sisters,
  and for all who serve the people of God,
  that they may be effective and tireless teachers
  of the good news of Jesus:
  let us pray to the Lord.

- For the nations and peoples of the world,
  that God's Spirit of understanding, charity, and peace
  may dwell in all human hearts:
  let us pray to the Lord.

- For the sick, the suffering, the recovering, and the dying,
  that the Spirit of love may be present to them
  in our compassionate care and support:
  let us pray to the Lord.

- For our deceased relatives and friends
  [especially _____ *],*
  that they may live forever in the light of God's peace:
  let us pray to the Lord.

- For the prayers we now offer in the silence of our hearts
  [Pause . . .]:
  let us pray to the Lord.

Gracious God, from you no secret is hidden;
every heart is open to you
and every wish is known.
Fill our hearts with the light of your Holy Spirit
that we may walk together united in faith
and grow in the strength of your love.
We make this prayer through Christ our Lord.

HOLY ORDERS

The Risen Christ is present in the midst of this holy assembly.
In humble confidence and joy, let us pray:

- For our Church and our diocese [parish],
  that we may be faithful to the priesthood of our baptism:
  let us pray to the Lord.

- For Pope N., Bishop N., and the bishops of our Church,
  that they may continue the mission
  entrusted by Jesus to the Twelve:
  let us pray to the Lord.

- For the priests and deacons of our Church,
  that they may be enablers of reconciliation
  and ministers of God's forgiveness:
  let us pray to the Lord.

- For those who serve, teach, and minister
  to the people of God,
  that their work may build up the Church
  into the body of Christ:
  let us pray to the Lord.

- For the nations and peoples of the world,
  that the peace and justice of God may reign in all lands:
  let us pray to the Lord.

- For the sick, the suffering, and the dying,
  that Christ the Healer may restore them
  to health and wholeness:
  let us pray to the Lord.

- For all who have died in the peace of Christ
  [especially _____],
  that they may find in the presence of God
  light, happiness, and peace:
  let us pray to the Lord.

- For the prayers we now make in the silence of our hearts
  [Pause . . .]:
  let us pray to the Lord.

We come to you in hope, O God,
knowing that you hear the prayers we offer in faith.
May your Spirit of wisdom and truth rest upon us always,
so that we may be prophets of your justice
and disciples of your love.
Grant these prayers we ask of you
in the name of your Son, our Lord Jesus Christ.

MARRIAGE

God is present in the midst of our celebration.
In faith, let us now pray for N. and N.,
as well as for all the people of God,
that we may all live together in God's love:

- For N. and N.,
  that God will bless their new life and home
  with peace and joy:
  let us pray to the Lord.

- For the parents of N. and N.,
  that God, the Father of all,
  will return to them abundantly
  the love and joy they have given to their children:
  let us pray to the Lord.

- For the families and friends of N. and N.,
  that they may continue to give them
  limitless support and unconditional love,
  especially in times of anxiety, pain, and despair:
  let us pray to the Lord.

- For our Church, the spouse of the Risen Christ,
  that our faithfulness to the gospel of love
  may make us the holy people of God:
  let us pray to the Lord.

- For our nation
  and for all the nations and peoples of the world,
  that the Spirit of God's love may reign over all the earth:
  let us pray to the Lord.

- For the sick, the poor, and the suffering,
  that the great love of God living in each one of us
  may restore them to health and hope:
  let us pray to the Lord.

- For our deceased relatives and friends
  [especially _____ *],*
  that they may rejoice forever
  at the wedding banquet of Christ the Bridegroom:
  let us pray to the Lord.

- For the prayers we now make in the silence of our hearts
  [Pause . . .]:
  let us pray to the Lord.

Gracious Father, Author of love,
hear our prayers for N. and N.
Be with them in their new life together
so that their marriage may be a living sacrament
of your loving presence in our midst.
We offer these prayers in the name of your Son,
your Love to us incarnate, Jesus Christ.

FOR THE FAITHFUL DEPARTED/
MASS OF CHRISTIAN BURIAL

To God, the Father of mercy and the Lord of compassion,
let us pray:

- For our Church and parish family,
  that we may be a community of hope
  in the promise of Jesus' resurrection:
  let us pray to the Lord.

- For the bishops, priests, deacons, and ministers
  who serve the Church,
  that their ministries among us
  may proclaim the good news of Jesus' resurrection:
  let us pray to the Lord.

- For the nations and peoples of the world,
  that God will destroy the hate that divides them
  and bring them together in justice and peace:
  let us pray to the Lord.

- For [the family of N. and for]
  all who mourn the deaths of loved ones,
  that, in our loving support
  they may find the strength to continue
  their own lives' journeys:
  let us pray to the Lord.

- For the poor, the suffering, the abused, and the forgotten,
  that they may have places of honor and welcome among us:
  let us pray to the Lord.

- For the sick, the recovering, and the dying,
  that the compassion of Jesus may be present to them
  in our prayers and care for them:
  let us pray to the Lord.

- For [N. and for] all who have died in Christ's peace,
  that they may find in the presence of God
  light, happiness, and peace:
  let us pray to the Lord.

- For the prayers we now make in the silence of our hearts
[Pause . . .]:
    let us pray to the Lord.

Hear our prayers, O Lord God
[as we gather to commend our brother/sister to you].
Transform our grief into hope,
fill the void we feel with your love,
comfort us with your promise of the Resurrection.
We make our prayers in the name of your Son,
our Risen Lord and Redeemer, Jesus Christ.